Before The First Codebreakers of the First World War

David Boyle

THE REAL PRESS
www.therealpress.co.uk

This edition published in 2016 by the Real Press, www.therealpress.co.uk © David Boyle

Ebook edition published in 2015 by Endeavour Press

The moral right of David Boyle to be identified as the authors of this work has been asserted by them in accordance with the Copyright, Designs and Patents Acts of 1988.

Some rights reserved. No part of this publication may be reproduced, stored in a retrieval system or transmitted in any form or by any means, electronic, mechanical or photocopying, recording, or otherwise for commercial purposes without the prior permission of the publisher. No responsibility can be accepted by the publisher for action taken as a result of information contained in this publication.

Cover design by Hodge Creative Ltd.

ISBN (print) 978-1523360253

For Fiona

"While some way that the Boche was not beaten by Foch
But by Winston or Ramsay Macdonald.
There are others who claim that the coup de grace came
From the Knoxes (our Dilly and Ronald)."
Frank Birch, Room 40 farewell party, 11 December 1918

Chapter 1
Before Enigma,
before Turing

It is wartime, and the stakes are high in the Atlantic and the North Sea. At the British fleet anchorage in the Orkneys, known to history as Scapa Flow, the signal lamps flash messages across the dank mist, unaware that they possess the most extraordinary weapon, utterly secret and also unprecedented in modern naval warfare. Unlike the wartime sailors of other generations, their most senior commanders can listen in to the hour-by-hour thoughts and orders of the other side and act accordingly. Not in the ships, perhaps, battling against the salt spray in the moment of battle, but via their own signals to the Admiralty. They can do so because of the invention of wireless telegraphy, but also because of the efforts of a handful of disparate amateurs who have forged themselves into the most successful team of cryptographers the world had ever known.

We can eavesdrop on their experience by listening to the reminiscences of Admiral Sir

William James, who had worked there under the legendary Captain 'Blinker' Hall:

"A visitor entering the rooms grouped around [Hall's] office at the Admiralty or being granted the rare privilege of passing through the door marked 'No admittance' which led to the cluster of rooms in the Old Building known as Room 40, was at once struck by the change of atmosphere. On his way through the long, bleak corridors, he had passed some elderly messengers, leisurely delivering papers to rooms from which there came no sound but the scratching of pens, and had caught a glimpse of solemn-looking officers, talking in whispers, and he now found himself in an atmosphere vibrating with excitement, expectations, urgency, friendship and high spirits... There was much to astonish a visitor to those rooms, and some excuse for his believing that he was the victim of a hoax. In Room 40, he would be introduced to a number of officers in RNVR uniform, and some, over military age, not in uniform, and [be] told that it real life they were fellows of colleges at Oxford and Cambridge, professors with a galaxy of academic distinctions, a director of the Bank of England, a famous music critic, a well-known actor, a publisher, an ex-president of the Oxford Union, an art expert, a world famous dress-designer. Perhaps his greatest surprise would be when he was introduced to a professor of divinity and a Roman Catholic priest in clerical garb... If he was lucky, Hall himself would come in like a tornado, and in his inimitable staccato way tell his staff, eagerly awaiting his return, what he had been doing..."

It sounds like Bletchley Park in its heyday, during the war of national survival, as Alan Turing, Peter Twinn, Hugh Alexander and their colleagues, wrestled with the complexities of the Nazi's naval Enigma code – but it isn't. It is what came before Bletchley, Turing or the cracking of Enigma, and what made them all possible – and arguably also what made them necessary. It was the peculiar assortment of people operating together to crack the German naval codes during the First World War, and known collectively as Room 40.

The scale was smaller, of course. Bletchley Park eventually employed as many as 10,000, three quarters of whom were women. The techniques were less sophisticated – they used logic and literary comparisons rather than mathematics and early computing. But even so, the people who launched Bletchley Park and shaped it, and who managed Turing and Twinn in the first two years of the Second World War, had learned their trade in Room 40 of the Old Admiralty Building in Whitehall, and absorbed their lessons about how codes could be cracked and then used from a man who was, in his own way, a genius of Turing proportions: Captain Reginald 'Blinker' Hall.

In those respects, Room 40 was the forerunner of Bletchley Park. It involved a series of near-fatal mistakes about how you should use decrypted information – about the best use of information in complex organisations – which were not made again as a result when the same team formed again on a wartime footing in 1939. They were not made partly because Blinker Hall gave detailed advice to Captain John Godfrey, who occupied his chair as Director of Naval Intelligence in 1939. They were also not made because so many people who were key to Room 40 were there to kickstart a similar operation, in much more difficult circumstances, at Bletchley Park.

Admiral James' description captures something of the spirit of the forerunners of Alan Turing and his colleagues. These were the days when codes were simpler and arguably easier to crack, when the wireless signals which carried them were barely understood, and when the whole of idea of taking down signals in code and learning to read them – in a systematic way – was only just being tried out in practice.

Not even the most far-sighted of those involved in cryptography in 1914, in either Britain or Germany, imagined that it might be possible to listen in to their enemy's naval signals systematically, and the team in Room 40 had to forge a whole new way of working to do so. Because Room 40 didn't just pave the way for Bletchley Park. It became Bletchley Park. The great personalities of the Government Code and Cypher School that became known as Station X, and the people who worked alongside Turing and the new generation had – many of them – begun their cryptographic careers in Room 40 in the bowels of the building which had presided over the fortunes of the navy since the days of Nelson. Frank Birch, Dilly Knox, Alastair Denniston were all, as young men, recruited to the peculiar mixture of individuals who floated in and around Room 40.

So if you ask how Enigma was cracked in the early years of the Second World War, there are various answers – gifted amateurism, the brilliance of Alan Turing, the very first computers, the pioneering work of Polish cryptographers. All those are true but there is one other crucial factor, which is much less well known. The same team had done it before. The techniques they developed then, the ideas that they came to rely on, the people they came to trust, had been developed the hard way, under intense pressure and absolute secrecy during World War I. This book tells their story and explains how they did it.

**

The story of how this varied and gifted group of men and women were forged into a successful cryptographic machine goes back to the first few days of the First World War, but it also contains a number of ironies given what was to come later.

For one thing, the Room 40 personnel represent the triumph of amateurism, in the best sense, in a deeply professional – not to say exclusive – environment. Other nations have achieved results differently. In the Second World War, the Germans relied overwhelmingly on professional naval officers as code-breakers. The Americans preferred to employ lawyers. The British bundled the whole lot of enthusiasts together, whether or not they knew any German or anything about the navy, and found that it worked. Their experience in Room 40 led to the same approach in Bletchley – indeed, it paved the way for the recruitment of Turing and others like him.

For another thing, the Room 40 team were barely recognised in their own lifetimes. They were prevented from writing their own accounts of their work between the wars, and then – thanks to the secrecy around Bletchley after the Second World War, most of them were dead by the time the truth began to emerge. We know about them partly because of recent work in what remains of the archives by modern historians, from biographies of them as individuals, and from a strange drama that

Frank Birch wrote after the Armistice in 1918, in the style of Alice in Wonderland, to celebrate the end of the war. But understanding that is itself a bit like cryptography.

We partly also know about their work by default. Malcolm Hay, who led the military cryptographic unit at MI1(b), burned all their records after the First World War. Memories of Room 40 have survived partly because of the extraordinary personality of their chief, 'Blinker' Hall, whose full role as never really been revealed.

There is a third irony, given what came later. Room 40 was so successful, eventually cracking a new cipher system every 24 hours – as opposed to a code (the distinction will be made plain later) – that it allowed the naval authorities to believe, quite mistakenly, that they would always master the business of naval codes.

The reverse was the case. Room 40 was so pre-eminent that it led to quite unwarranted over-confidence among the British naval authorities in the next generation. In my book *Operation Primrose*, I explain how the roles of the two nations' naval cryptographers were reversed in the Second World War. For nearly four years of the war, the German cryptographers at B-Dienst were able to read virtually all the British naval wireless signals, having cracked the code back in 1935. It was only later that the British admiralty, like the German admiralty in the latter stages of the First World War, grasped that their signals traffic was vulnerable.

But then again, Enigma was different. It required a mathematical approach, which was not usually used in Room 40. Indeed it required Alan Turing to invent modern computers to master the problem, and that was not something that the old hands from Room 40 had ever really encountered before. It was to cause huge difficulties, in different ways, for both Denniston and Knox.

Then there is a final irony. The failures of the early years of the First World War, where – thanks partly to Winston Churchill – the secret of Room 40 was kept so obsessively, and the benefits of reading the enemy's signals protected so overwhelmingly, that it led to major failures in operations at sea, notably at the Battle of Jutland in 1916.

This was the same mistake the Nazis made in the Second World War, dividing their cryptography staff, keeping secrets so obsessively that they became more concerned about traitors within than enemy cryptographers without. Because Denniston, Knox, Birch and their colleagues had been through the First World War, they knew the mistakes that had been made and were in a position to make sure – by 1939 – that the right structures were in place to use the information that had been gleaned so laboriously.

Those lessons were learned the hard way. In fact, the whole story of Room 40 and the genius of Hall and his high risk, low profile, not to say devious approach to espionage, were also an object lesson for modern corporations and how to share information – and to do so without the secrets leaking out. It was a tremendously twentieth century problem – how to manage vast organisations, but still provide as much information as possible up and down the hierarchy. The First World War ran slap up against the problem in almost every aspect of the war effort, but Hall and the cryptographers managed to hammer out a way forward, and did so in such a way that the same people could use it to win a generation later against the Nazis.

It was a difficult problem but, by 1918, they had begun to master it, just in time to counteract the real threat to national survival in both world wars – the U-boat challenge to the nation's supply routes.

**

It was a peculiar place to be, the Admiralty Building, at the beating heart of empire and umbilically connected by phone lines to the Grand Fleet at their wartime anchorage in Scapa Flow, and by other lines and cables to the outposts across the world. Remote from the sea and spray and splash of shells, just as it was remote in some ways from the roar of the

Western Front, there was a danger, for any of the cryptographers and the burgeoning staff of Room 40, that they might at any moment be handed a white feather for shirking danger. It was one reason they were all eventually given ranks and uniforms in the Royal Naval Volunteer Reserve.

In another sense, Whitehall was the very centre of the war effort, and those who escaped briefly for lunch passed the ambulances and nurses taking the wounded direct from the front off the trains at Charing Cross, with the Flanders mud still on their uniforms. From two days after the declaration of war, they were also passing posters that declared 'Your King and Country Need YOU' in a big red border. The famous Kitchener poster first appeared in November.

Walking round the immediate vicinity from the Admiralty, on their way to wrestle with the naval codes, took them also past the queues outside the Central Recruiting Office in Old Scotland Yard, and – in the other direction – the tented village that grew up so quickly in Horse Guards Parade for recruitment, or the recruitment office in St Martin's-in-the-Fields in Trafalgar Square.

They would see, not just the ferocious women in boa hats distributing white feathers to the civil servants, or listen to Hallie Miles singing 'Oh, we don't want to lose you' at her husband's expensive Trafalgar Square restaurant, the Chandos. They would see the offices of the |German shipping line Nordeutscher Lloyd in Cockspur Street boarded up and plastered with recruitment posters, and the other shops draped in union jacks.

They would wait impatiently for buses, now that 350 of them had been sent out to Belgium from London, and equally impatiently for taxis, because so many of them had been converted into ambulances. As the weeks went by and war became more familiar, they would see the lines of Kitchener's new army drilling in St James's Park, past the lake that had been drained to its muddy bottom in case it glinted in the moonlight and attracted zeppelins.

The nights were particularly strange, with the streets darkened – the traffic accidents doubled in London in the first months of the blackout. The advertising lights were dark and the theatre performances were earlier. The restaurants and clubs were half empty now that people were going to bed earlier. So many waiters had been German or Austrian that it was also difficult to staff them as they had been before the war. There was a gun on the roof of the Foreign Office and searchlights sweeping the sky at night.

"London is a curious place now," said the novelist Henry Rider Haggard, who was to play a peculiar role himself in Room 40. "The lighting is about as bright only as that which I remember as a boy, when the gas lamps were few and burned dully and electric lamps were unknown."

The West End, just a few minutes away, was still a potentially disordered and dangerous place. There were nearly 900 arrests there after the riots that followed the sinking of the *Lusitania*, which coincided with the first zeppelin raids. The zeppelin threat was uppermost in the mind of many policy-makers and at the Admiralty in particular, because air defence was their responsibility, just as balloon raids came under the auspices of the German navy. As Jackie Fisher – head of the navy as First Sea Lord – became more querulous, he urged a policy that one German intern should be executed for everyone killed in air raids. He threatened to resign if it wasn't put to the cabinet, where Churchill persuaded his colleagues to reject the idea.

But the biggest sign that the nation was at war was not so much the fact that passers-by were continually wearing black. It was the continuing activity, day and night, at Charing Cross Hospital. The traffic there slowed down as it went past the huge red cross flying from the flagstaff and the enormous white banner which read: QUIET – FOR THE WOUNDED.

It was hard not to be aware, if you were one of the select few, commuting to your cryptographic shift at Room 40, that London was at war.

Chapter 2
Magdeburg

If any one person was responsible for the advent of wireless cryptography, and the military decision which made it possible, it was perhaps Major Adrian Grant Duff, on secondment from the Black Watch in the years before the First World War to the Committee of Imperial Defence. It was Grant Duff who wrote eight of the nine chapters of the War Book, the comprehensive cross-governmental plan for mobilisation in the event of war.

He was to be killed in the first weeks of the war, leading the Black Watch at the Battle of the Aisne, but by then the War Book had moved smoothly into action and one of those imaginative preparations which had been included was the idea of cutting the underwater cables that connected Germany with the outside world. Accordingly, when war was declared on 4 August 1914, a cable ship called the *Telconia* was waiting near the spot on the high seas where five telephone cables ran from the frontier between Germany and the Netherlands near Emden, down the English Channel to France, Spain, Africa and the Americas. Using a grappling iron dragged along the ocean floor the following day, they caught the cables and cut them.

There was one more link which crossed the Mediterranean to Liberia and thence to Brazil, but that was in British hands, and the company was persuaded very quietly to cut it some months later. Germany was cut from the secure telegraphic system that criss-crossed the world. It meant that their main signals would have to go via wireless, if they were going to be sent at all, or perhaps via diplomatic traffic via a neutral country – which would mean routing the cable via London. Wireless was anyway increasingly important for naval communications, though it had only been introduced at sea in 1897, and the Wireless Telegraphy branch of the Royal Navy had been launched only eight years before the war. Now, diplomatic signals would have to go the same way.

What wireless could and couldn't do, the extent to which it could be overheard or travel great distances, was little understood, even by the experts. Nor had the War Book really thought through the implications of cutting the German cables. It suddenly made codes supremely important.

One of the controversies about the history of Room 40 was how much the British authorities had thought about codes before 1914. They had certainly not prepared for sheer flood of coded, intercepted signals that would pour into the Admiralty or War

Office. But recent scholarship suggests that they had in fact been making preparations to intercept and, in a quiet way, have a go at code-breaking, but the whole story had been reduced before to an amateur series of lucky coincidences.

There was probably some truth in both sides, but it does seem to have occurred to the British that the codes would arrive and that it might be possible, in some rare circumstances, to listen in and even to understand them. They may even have made some early contacts with some of the individuals who might help them do so. We can only guess. Either way, on the first day of the war, or possibly the second, an historic lunch took place between the new Director of Naval Intelligence, Rear-Admiral Henry Oliver and his old friend the Director of Naval Education, Sir Alfred Ewing.

It seems unlikely that this was a long-standing arrangement, despite what they said later. It is hard to believe Oliver dashed off for lunch on the first day of the war unless there was a very pressing reason for him to do so. Nonetheless, he clearly did, and they met at the United Services Club in Pall Mall. "It struck me," said Oliver later, perhaps disingenuously, "that this was the very man I wanted."

It was an important lunch. Oliver was a workaholic, who rarely left his office, and taciturn to the point of rudeness. He was so silent he was known in the navy as 'Dummy'. Since he slept by his desk, he was also said to be, with his bushy eyebrows and shaggy beard, the worst-dressed officer in the fleet. His friend Ewing had a high reputation as an educationalist. He had been brought into the Admiralty by the modernising firebrand Sir John Fisher, when he was First Sea Lord the first time – the operational head of the navy before the war – to professionalise naval education, and had done so with great flair. Ewing's significance now was that his hobby happened to be codes and puzzles.

Early in the lunch, one assumes, Oliver popped the question. Could he help out for a few months, just until the war was over – widely believed to be in a few week's time – and see what could be done by way of breaking the German naval codes? Ewing agreed on the spot, and it seems likely that this had always been the plan.

In the few days that followed, Ewing visited places where there were codes he could look at: the British Museum reading room, the Post Office and the Lloyd's of London. His other great advantage in charge of naval education was that he also had access to the naval colleges, which were then very conveniently on vacation. Within a few days, he had roped in a number of them to help out. In this half-hearted, amateur way, the great secret institutions which launched the careers of Knox and Turing and all the others began life.

One of the first to help out was Alastair Denniston, later head of the Government Codes and Cipher School and in charge of Bletchley Park at the outbreak of war in 1939, and an Olympic hockey player. He was teaching German at Osborne Naval College, and he was one of the first to be involved. Ewing also spread his net a little further than Osborne and Dartmouth, tracking down and inveigling a diplomat, Lord Herschell, also a well-known collector of Persian armour, and Robert Norton, a former Foreign Office official, then living in what had been Henry James's old home, Lamb House in Rye.

For the time being, all Denniston and colleagues had by way of resources was a corner of Ewing's office at the Admiralty and in practice – since their presence was both unofficial and top secret – they had to dodge into the small corner which Ewing's secretary used if anybody came in.

Ewing's next mission was to beef up the ability of the navy to listen in to wireless traffic. It transpired – though we have to take this with another pinch of salt – that one of his friends was an enthusiastic radio ham, and had been doing exactly that, in flagrant defiance of the Defence of the Realm Act. This was the barrister Russell Clarke; the story suggests that he tied the Post Office officials in such legal knots that they just let him get on with it. A similar amateur radio sleuth turned out to be the Somerset landowner Colonel Baynton Hippisley. Modern historians have assumed that actually Clarke, and possibly Hippisley, may actually have been working semi-officially for the War Office.

Clarke told Ewing that he reckoned the best site for a wireless listening post would probably be Hunstanton Lifeboat Station on the Norfolk coast. The two friends roped in a third, Leslie Lambert, later well-known as the BBC announcer A. J. Alan, a keen radio amateur and amateur conjurer. Together they rigged up an antenna on the roof at Hunstanton and began listening in. To do so they organised themselves and their friends into eight-hour shifts, and provided their services both to the Admiralty and War Office.

Meanwhile, the War Office cryptographers at MI1(b) were also gearing up, though we know less about their activities because all their records were destroyed at the end of the war, under retired Brigadier General Francis Anderson, a mathematician who had been in charge of tapping Boer telegrams during the South African war. Anderson forged close relationships with the French military cryptographers, but the French were about to make the opposite mistake to the British. A decrypted signal revealed that the Kaiser was visiting a sector of the Western Front in Belgium. The French artillery battered the sector, without managing to hit the German emperor, but the news of the decrypt leaked out to *Le Matin,* which boasted about the bombardment. Not surprisingly, the Germans army changed their codes.

The British military and naval authorities were also about to fall out with each other. There had been a great deal of co-operation between the two services in the first weeks of war and the Hunstanton Lifeboat Station was among the fruits of that relationship. But Clarke wandered into the Admiralty one day and suggested a weekend trial of listening in to the less powerful German naval transmitters. Ewing wasn't keen, but agreed to try and the test was a huge success. Suddenly a whole world opened up for them. The air was alive with signals which they had no idea could reach so far before. The signals were loud and clear and directed towards the German fleet base of Wilhelmshaven from their naval transmitter at Norddeich. By trial and error, Clarke, Hippisley and Lambert found themselves listening directly to wireless signals to and from the High Seas Fleet itself.

The Hunstanton station became the core of what became known in the Second World War as the Y service, the wireless interception and tracking service, and – together with the Post Office – they were eventually able to intercept enemy naval signals systematically. The difficulty for inter-service co-operation was that this was now so important to the Admiralty, at least potentially – if they could find a way of understanding the signals – that they pulled rank as the Senior Service. Hunstanton was to be used exclusively for listening to naval signals. No discussion was allowed. As a result, the War Office withdrew its co-operation. Nobody tried to dissuade them.

**

All that time, Denniston and the other new cryptographers were making a little progress under the Ewing's guidance, aware that what they really needed was some kind of key to the incomprehensible signals filled with jumbled numbers that they were receiving. In fact, the week after the beginning of the war, the first breakthrough had already taken place, off the Australian coast near Melbourne.

This was a stroke of genius by the Royal Australian Navy, aware that the steamship *Hobart* was a German ship and was apparently unaware that war had been declared. Captain John Richardson and his boarding party stopped the ship and went aboard wearing civilian clothes, and pretending to be quarantine inspectors. Richardson was aware that there would come a time – if they were patient enough – when the *Hobart*'s captain realised what was happening, and he would try to destroy his naval code books. He was watched secretly the whole time and, sure enough, in the early hours of the next morning, he slipped out of bed and slid back a secret panel. Richardson was there in a moment, pistol drawn and the German codes were in Australian hands.

They turned out to include the code known as HVB (*Handeslverkehrsbuch*) which was used between the German Admiralty and their merchant ships, and was sometimes used within the German High Seas Fleet as well. It was an absolutely vital find, if it could be got to Ewing and his colleagues in London.

The only problem was that Richardson's superiors were not as imaginative as he was. They were pleased of course, but they failed to inform the Admiralty in London until 9 September, nearly a month later. Then they sent the precious cargo to London by ship which eventually arrived at the end of October.

In their defence, we have to remember that this was a different age, more than a century ago now, and the systems and technologies were not widely understood. Knowledge about what instantaneous communication meant in practice in naval warfare had not filtered far, even through the senior ranks of the military, and the navy retained their traditional bias against new technologies. Time after time, officers assumed that the admirals above them were as omniscient as they believed themselves to be. All too often, they remained silent about new information, and failed to get basic intelligence either to their superiors on at sea or to the Admiralty in London. The *Hobart* incident was only the first of many. They were symptoms of the emergence of a whole new dispensation.

In any case, by the time the code books from Australia had arrived in London, the success of Captain Richardson and his men had been overshadowed by another breakthrough, which was one of the most famous, controversial and mysterious incidents of the war. It took place as early as 26 August.

**

In the first few days of the war, the German light cruiser *Breslau* had given British forces in the Mediterranean the slip and helped bring Turkey into the war on the German side, by sailing down the Dardanelles and into Constantinople.

Eighteen days later, her sister ship, the brand new *Magdeburg,* was in company with other units off the coast of what is now Estonia, in thick fog and suffering from mechanical difficulties. One of the three turbines had broken down and the ship was anyway not fully operational. It was at this point that she ran aground close to the entrance to the Gulf of Finland. There was an attempt to take her in tow, but it was soon clear that *Magdeburg* was stuck fast, and dangerously close to the Russian navy. The destroyer V26 came alongside to take off the crew and the captain began the process of destroying the confidential papers and codebooks, and setting explosive charges to blow up the ship, before it could fall into enemy hands.

The bad luck continued. The fog began to lift and, in the distance, there suddenly appeared the two Russian cruisers *Pallada* and *Bogatyr*, belching smoke and approaching fast. Confusion reigned. The explosive charges went off accidentally and soon the captain and 56 crew members were prisoners of the Russians and a number of copies of the key to one of the most important German naval codes were in Russian hands.

It was never quite clear how this happened. There are stories about the codebooks being clutched in the dead hands of a drowned sailor, being thrown overboard and rescued, or simply – as the Russians said – found in the sinking charthouse of the *Magdeburg*. "Well, splinters are bound to fly at a time like this," the Kaiser is reported to have said when he heard about the loss, but he did not appreciate – and neither did senior staff at the German admiralty – that the codebooks had fallen into enemy hands, though there were warnings inside the German navy that this was precisely what had happened.

The Russians had an enlightened and generous approach to their stroke of luck. They offered one copy to the British, on condition that they should send a ship to collect it. Accordingly, the old cruiser *Theseus* was sent from Scapa Flow to Alexandrovsk, and – just as there had been with the *Hobart* – there was then a long delay. It wasn't until 30 September, partly waiting for six trunks of clothes belonging to the wife of the First Sea Lord, Prince Louis of Battenberg, that the *Theseus* set sail for home.

The new codebook did not arrive at the Admiralty in London until 13 October. It turned out to be the code known as SKM (*Signalbuch der Kaiserlichen Marine*), which was the one they used for major operations and it was massive. The book itself was six inches thick and measured fifteen inches by twelve inches. It would take a lot of work to plough through and use, but it was at least a start.

The third stroke of luck which kick-started the cryptographers in London took place four days later, off the Dutch coast, when the British cruiser *Undaunted* and accompanying escorts ran suddenly into four old German destroyers and, after a short action, sank them. At least one box containing the codebooks was thrown over the side, and what happened next, like the other stories, have to be taken with yet another pinch of salt – it is hardly clear whether these are real accounts or stories made up later to cover up the skulduggery involved in seizing the codes. But, that proviso out of the way, it is said that, six weeks later, a British trawler pulled up a box in the same area which proved to contain the codebooks for the VB code, the *Verkehrsbuch*, used to communicate between flag officers and the army and other units.

However this really happened, the incident was known later to the Room 40 team as "the miraculous draught of fishes".

**

As we have seen, the first of these keys which arrived, dried out and ready to use, was the SKB code from the *Magdeburg*, straight down by train from Scotland once the *Theseus* returned to port. It is probably fair to say that Ewing's first cryptographers had made little or no progress in their first month or so of operation. But even with this major key, it turned out not to be straightforward at all.

In those days, wireless signal codes worked rather as they did in the age of signal flags and sail. The words or phrases were in numbered groups, usually of five figures. The first numbers usually referred to the page of the codebook where the phrase was listed, the next number to the column and then the numbered code. It meant that signals could be pretty short, reducing the time the wireless was running, unless they were complex instructions or introducing orders that were very specific to the situation.

In Nelson's day, he was encouraged to change the word of his famous signal 'England expects that every man will do his duty', because 'expects' was in the flag signal book but the word the originally wanted – 'confides' – would have to be spelled out. It was the same a century later. Find the numbered code and you should be able to work out the phrase. In fact, without the codebook, it would have been next to impossible to work out from scratch, until the basic pattern became clear.

SKM had more complicated arrangements: three-letter codes for different orders and – if the order wasn't in the book – there would be a warning code and then it would be spelled out in a substitution table, another relic from the days when these things would have been done with signal flags. This substitute list included Greek numbers and ship's names were another complication: they were spelled out with a *beta*, followed by two letters from the list.

But it was hardly a matter of just looking the codes up. It was pretty clear, once the SKM codebook was in British hands, that the signals were not just coded but also enciphered. Codes substitute whole phrases with numbers or letters. The German navy then added an extra layer using a cipher for each number, so that each one stood for something else, using another key that the Room 40 team clearly did not possess.

Part of the problem, as Ewing rightly identified, was that none of the disparate band of individuals he had managed to beg, borrow or steal knew much about the navy or naval procedures. He asked Oliver for a German naval expert and was given Paymaster-Commander Charles Rotter, who shifted his desk into Ewing's secretary's tiny office, along with everyone else. It was Rotter who noticed that the signals from the Norddeich transmitter had been numbered and that these numbers had also been ciphered. It did not take too long to put them in some kind of order and so the cipher key began to take shape after all. Rotter's first successes came with weather reports, which are always the easiest because o the frequently repeated words and phrases.

Later in the war, the German naval cipher would be changed every day at midnight, and it was the duty of the night duty team to crack it before daybreak. But that was some years ahead. Just for now, the cipher was more or less in place, thanks to some trial and error, and the signals were finally beginning to be readable.

It was also beginning to be clearer which code applied to which message. HVB was used by zeppelins and U-boats, both under naval control, and so would turn out to be increasingly important as the war progressed, and the idea that there might be a great fleet action began to fade into the distance. VB was by far the most effective code, used mainly to communicate with embassies abroad, but for embassies there was an extra problem: the numbers were in a five numeral code system, and these numbers were then jumbled up according to a complex system known to the Germans as *Chi*, so that it looked random. In fact, Chi set out a code at the beginning of each message which allowed the German side to know where to start putting the numbers into a piece of squared paper, from where the message could then be read off horizontally.

This was a challenge for Room 40, just getting to grips with the patterns of the wireless messages for the first time. They were helped because, unlike the German army command, the German admiralty was surprisingly relaxed about the loss of the *Magdeburg*. Despite the warnings by enlightened officers, it was not until February 1915, six months after the ship went down, that Henry of Prussia, naval commander-in-chief in the Baltic and the Kaiser's brother, wrote to the High Seas Fleet commander that "it must be assumed with virtual certainty that these charts were fished up by the Russians, who came on the scene immediately afterwards. It is probable that an SKM key simultaneously fell into the hands of the Russians". Even then, the German admiralty failed to provide the new code that he had requested.

**

While all this had been going on, a small earthquake had been happening at the Admiralty. The First Sea Lord, Prince Louis of Battenberg, Lord Mountbatten's father, had been forced out by a xenophobic public campaign that objected to a man with a German name being privy to the naval secrets of the empire. Battenberg was also in great pain from gout and, though a brilliant administrator, was not the energetic, dogmatic driver that Fisher had been – and his political boss, Winston Churchill, had anyway hoped to replace him with Fisher on the outbreak of war.

It was a traumatic time for the navy, and during the brief inter-regnum before Fisher was recalled from retirement, at the querulous age of 73, there had been an embarrassing confrontation outside Ewing's office. One of his new cryptographic staff, without a uniform, had refused to admit the Assistant Secretary to Ewing's Admiralty. There was a terrible fuss, and after which – when calmer heads prevailed – it was clear that you could hardly run a cryptographic service from a small cubby hole. Instead, they were offered Room 40. It was only 24 foot by 17 foot, but it was at least theirs. It was found at the end of the main corridor at the Admiralty, by tall windows looking out to the west, across the garden of 10 Downing Street over St James's Park and Horse Guards Parade. It was also later the operational office of the Director of Naval Intelligence in the Second World War as well, and James Bond's creator Ian Fleming guarded the door to it.

Then the old man returned. The old sparring partners, Churchill and Fisher had huge admiration for each other's dynamism and reforming zeal, and Fisher was soon initiated into the great secret of what was now Room 40. They were beginning to be able to read the enemy's naval signals.

Fisher was only to last in office for a few short months, though they were crucial ones. Churchill would not survive much longer but, in their first few days together, they discussed how this extraordinary benefit might be used and what the procedure ought to be. Oliver was being promoted to chief of the Admiralty War Staff, to be replaced as intelligence chief, but by the time his replacement had taken up his post, the damage had been done. The procedure for using the great secret was, as it turned out, a terrible mistake.

Churchill and Fisher wrote a joint memo which said that all decoded messages should be logged into a book which was kept under lock and key, and all the other related paperwork should be burned. The new director of naval intelligence, Captain Reginald Hall, plays a key part in this story. He arrived just in time to suggest a variation: that the log book should not be carried around but two copies should be made – one for the director of the intelligence division (himself) and one for the Admiralty's chief of staff (Oliver).

The scene was set for a monumental failure to use the intelligence well, and the problem stemmed from the original conversation between Oliver and Ewing at the United Services Club. The idea of breaking codes was a kind of amateur jape, without much hope of success. At that stage, the logic of success had not really occurred to them. They had no idea that the entire weight of enemy signals traffic might soon be available to them and could be used on a systematic basis, if they were equipped to do use it. It didn't occur to Churchill or Fisher and nor did it occur to Oliver, who treated the decrypts like a personal source designed to inform his signals to the fleet.

The problem was partly that Ewing was responsible to nobody and now had no official relationship to Hall, Oliver's replacement as intelligence director. Ewing was 'too distinguished a man to be placed officially under the orders of the Director of Intelligence or Chief of Staff," said Oliver.. His chosen staff had little or no naval experience or expertise and Churchill's memo meant that the signals secrets were now guarded so closely that the results could not be useful. It was not a mistake that the same people would make in the Second World War.

Yet Oliver did see the problem of the lack of naval knowledge among the new team, and he acted to tackle it. He was probably made forcefully aware of it by his crustier colleagues, who took against the idea of signals decrypts, and contributed to the internal secrecy that had been forced on the new source. He would appoint a serving naval officer to look through the signals and make notes about their significance, so that the information could be passed on effectively to the Admiralty chart room, which was kept up to date with what knowledge there was about German fleet dispositions. As a result, Commander Herbert Hope was whisked from his job elsewhere in the intelligence department, much to his disappointment – he had been hoping to go back to sea – and found himself posted to another desk job. Hope found himself effectively cut off from Room 40 because of the internal secrecy, and shunned by the admirals, and was given almost no information that might allow him to understand what he was supposed to do.

It was an obsessive secrecy which meant that the full benefits from knowing what the signals meant could never be banked. Worse, it brought the whole intelligence from the Admiralty to the fleet at sea into disrepute. When individual naval commanders on their bridges at sea had no idea of the significance of what they were being told, they would often ignore it, even when it was both vital and accurate. The verdict by one post-war expert on German signals security was that they "elaborately hid from subordinates facts and intentions which at least for three quarters of the war, they failed to conceal from the enemy". This probably applied to both sides, though on the German side it was made worse by the fact that – before the war – nobody had any idea just how powerful their wireless transmitters could be: their high power transmitter signals could be picked up as far away as China, so they could certainly be heard by a small group of friends sheltering on the roof of a lifeboat station in Norfolk.

The British navy preferred the old system of flags and signal lamps, but in the height of battle these could not always be accurate or effective, as they found to their cost at the Battle of Dogger Bank in 1915. The central problem was that listening in to signals and cracking the codes was so unexpected, for both sides, that it was regarded by Churchill and Fisher as something so extraordinary, a jewel of great price that could and would barely ever be used. In fact, by the end of the war, 20,000 wireless signals had poured into Room 40 and most of them were successfully decoded.

By 1918, the British had not just cracked the codes, they had understood by trial and error what kind of operational structures were needed to make sure the information contained in the decrypts could be used effectively. It was a lesson that, despite the slumbers of the interwar years, they did not forget – and which led to the successful struggle with Enigma and the successes of Turing and his colleagues. It even led, through them, to the development of modern computers. But the fact that the lessons were learned and made effective, and that Room 40 was transformed into the modern espionage agency that it became, was largely down to one man. The legendary Captain Reginald 'Blinker' Hall.

Chapter 3
Churchill

Henry Oliver's new job as Chief of the Admiralty Staff and naval assistant to the First Lord of the Admiralty kept the old workaholic chained to his desk. He insisted on drafting all the signals to the fleet himself, which meant he had to be present as close as possible to 24 hours a day. It was a punishing and exhausting ordeal.

His first task in the morning was to attempt to control his political boss, who was the unusually uncontrollable Winston Churchill, First Lord of the Admiralty since 1911. He would knock on the door of one of the seven bedrooms maintained at the Admiralty, a and there the First Lord would be, sitting up in bed, smoking a large cigar, making a range of immediate demands. Next, he made his way down to the chart room and moved the ship counters on the map which was kept for the edification of visiting dignitaries. The real map, covered up at the side of the room, would then have to be adjusted correctly.

Then he would look at the signals intelligence. Because he had been instrumental in launching Room 40, he continued to behave as if it was, in the words of one intelligence officer later, "Oliver's private cryptographic bureau". He failed to integrate that information with first-hand knowledge from admirals who were on the spot, just as he failed to discuss his conclusions with the cryptographers or other intelligence staff. When he misinterpreted the raw data, the local admirals – Jellicoe or Beatty in the Battlecruiser Force – would see that it contradicted what they could see through their own binoculars and they dismissed it, then and later, because they had no idea what the source was.

In fact, just nine people were initiated at that stage into the secret outside Room 40. They included the First Lord, Fisher (the First Sea Lord, the operational head), Oliver (the chief of staff), Wilson (his predecessor brought back from retirement), Hall (the new director of naval intelligence), and finally Sir John Jellicoe, the commander-in-chief in Scapa Flow, who was still furiously asking for a copy of the *Magdeburg* code book well into December 1914. The prime minister seems not to have been told. As for, Commander Hope, whose task was to sift the decrypts and interpret them, he only saw a handful come across his desk every day. He wrote hopeful notes on them and wondered what happened to them next.

The stage was then set for Oliver's successor as intelligence director to emerge on the scene. Hall was known as 'Blinker', because of his habit of blinking his eyes, one of the peculiar physical survivals of a traumatic period in his childhood when he was at a military boarding school, and where pupils were so badly fed that they had to steal turnips from neighbouring farms. He was a bold innovator as commanding officer of the new battlecruiser *Queen Mary*, where he had introduced new four-hour watches, which were now being adopted for the whole navy. He had abolished the ship's police, the first commanding officer to do so, and set up a ship's chapel and a ship's cinema for the first time. He was hugely respected by Beatty, his own admiral, but nobody could have been more disappointed than Hall himself when his health broke down in the first few weeks of the war – it isn't clear how – and he asked to be relieved of his command.

The decision probably saved his life. Only twenty were saved from the North Sea when *Queen Mary* blew up at a critical moment in the Battle of Jutland eighteen months later. But it also meant that the Admiralty gained one of the most extraordinary minds ever to go into naval intelligence, with ambitions and aspirations that went way beyond what might be legitimately classed as naval interests. Hall tracked down spies, engaged in dirty tricks, sent fake messages, double-crossed double agents, oversaw a whole series of different theatres from his teeming brain – even personally and successfully intervening to bring the USA into the war when he saw an opportunity to do so.

The American ambassador Walter Page was a particular admirer, describing him as a genius: "for Hall can look through you and see the very muscular movements of your immortal soul while he is talking to you". There is no doubt also that, unlike some of his contemporaries who were heroic commanders at sea, Hall had luck on his side. He took the most extraordinary risks with his career, offering the Turks £4 million to let the allied fleet down the Dardanelles, on his own initiative, having an important double agent murdered for fear that he would give away the great cryptography secret. He also leaked copies of the captured Irish revolutionary Roger Casement's 'black diaries', filled with lurid homosexual fantasies, to the press to undermine the campaign to have his execution reprieved.

Hall was extremely popular with his staff, generated the most extraordinary loyalty, despite occasional explosions of temper, but his ruthlessness was legendary. One story was the result of his rage that a German spy he had been instrumental in capturing was only given a light sentence on the grounds, according to Mr Justice Bray, that he had not succeeded in damaging anywhere of military importance. Hall went back to the office, organised for a message to be sent out in the name of another double agent which listed the judge's home address as a munitions factory. When it was duly bombed in a zeppelin raid, and the judge had only just escaped with his life, Hall arranged to sit next to him at a dinner, listened to his traumatic story, and then said: "Ah well, at least it wasn't a target of military importance".

The story was told as an example of Hall's sardonic humour. It is just as much a demonstration of his ability to fight what was, in some ways, a private war, organised using rules developed by himself, unacknowledged and barely seen by anyone in authority. That was how he worked, writing little down, making up the occasional story to justify his actions or to obscure Room 40's methods. In doing so, he virtually reinvented modern espionage.

He would also do anything for his friends. "Steal petrol!" he was overheard to order one of his assistants when a friend of his had run out of fuel in Whitehall, during the period when petrol was most controlled. The tank was filled within ten minutes.

Hall was a force of nature. Subtle, clever, intoxicating and extraordinarily distinctive – he looked like Mr Punch – Hall burst onto the unsuspecting Admiralty. Ewing was still nominally in charge of Room 40, and so Hall had no authority there, at least not officially, but clearly the situation could not last.

He took up his post on 14 October 1914, and immediately set to work. It was not his responsibility that Commander Hope was all but isolated, still cursing his poor luck for eking out his time writing notes on the six signals that reached him every day. He told Hall that what he really needed was to talk directly to the cryptographers and of course he did. Hall could hardly order it, but the situation was increasingly frustrating as his first weeks went by in the job.

What seems to have happened instead is that he suggested that Lord Herschell, later head of Room 40's diplomatic section, should run accidentally into Fisher, and claim he couldn't find Hope to whom he was delivering messages. Whatever anyone might claim about Fisher later – his vainglorious mixture of violent pugnacity and querulous demands – he was no snob. He could and did talk to anyone. "Looking for Hope?" he said. "I know where he is; come on, I'll show you". Fisher and Herschell's arrival gave Hope the opportunity he needed to demonstrate to the man at the top the difficulties he was having. Fisher listened and acted, and ordered Herschel to visit Hope twice a day with copies of all the messages.

"I was initiated into the Mystery on 16 November 1914," Hope wrote later. He became an absolutely vital link between the formal intelligence world and the cryptographers, sifting the signals and choosing what was crucial. He spoke no German but developed a kind of sixth sense about what was important. Once he had been allowed to know the story of the *Magdeburg*, he could be useful in other ways too. German ships broadcast their position using coded map squares and there had been a key seized along with the other papers taken from there. Hope settled down immediately and plotted all the positions that had been revealed in the decrypted messages. It was immediately clear that some of the grid squares were never used by enemy ships, and it might be possible to make an educated guess that these were minefields. Hope plotted the minefields and had the maps circulated to ships at sea.

Soon Room 40 came to be dominated by the authority of Hope and Rotter, who were always there between 9am and 7pm, Hope dealing with the translated signals and Rotter looking at the fragments he could understand and working out what was important to prioritise for the cryptographers. Anything that was completely obscure went into a huge tin box marked 'NSL', which stood for 'neither sent nor logged'.

Hope was also a pioneer, in his own way. He realised that some messages included routine codes and some did not. When the codes were not routine, it may well mean that the orders were part of some major operation. He made it his job to work out when these non-routine codes were being used. But he also realised that the Admiralty was using their decoded messages defensively. They were being used to warn of offensive operations by the enemy and to anticipate them. Since the war was rapidly developing as a defensive one at sea, Hope realised that they would have to develop techniques for using the decrypts *offensively* – so that they could begin to take the war to the enemy in harbour. It was very much Hall's thinking too.

One of the problems with writing about Room 40, especially as a pioneer for Bletchley Park, is that Hall was operating, not just outside the law, but outside all conventions. He kept his ruses in his head, managed them by force of personality and his own charm, and wrote very little down. In the years after the war, he tried to deflect the real story over and over again by inventing little untruths and obscurities. So we will probably never know, for example, if it was Hall's fake signal to Admiral Maximilian von Spee's squadron in the Pacific which lured them so disastrously to the Falklands, where the battlecruisers *Invincible* and *Inflexible* lay in wait.

But we do know more about the fleet action that so nearly took place a few days after the battle of the Falkland Isles in December 1914, because it was the first naval action of any kind where one side was able, and with some clarity, to listen in to the thoughts, preparations and orders of the other.

**

This might be the moment to explain the origin of the idea of 'battlecruisers' which were to play such a role in this and the other actions in the North Sea. It was originally Fisher's idea to launch a new class of warship that was as big, or bigger, than a capital ship – a conventional battleship – but was faster and therefore less well protected. They would be "stronger than anything faster and faster than anything stronger". Their high point was the successful destruction of Von Spee's squadron in the South Atlantic. After that, they tended to be used as fast scouting units ahead of the battlefleet, which took them into conflict with other battlecruisers, for which they had no really been designed. The British battlecruisers, sleek, vast and beautiful and under the command of the dashing Sir David Beatty, lay at anchor in the Firth of Forth, so that they could speed south to prevent the bombardment of English seaside towns by units of the German High Seas Fleet.

In fact, it was the German battlecruisers which sent the first signal which alerted Room 40 that something was being planned. It was sent by the commander of their battlecruiser scouting force, Admiral Franz Ritter von Hipper, on 14 December.

He was asking for air reconnaissance over a sector of the North Sea and revealing that his force would leave the Jade Estuary at 0330. The signal was successfully decoded and, at 7pm, Admiral Sir Arthur Wilson – known to the navy as Old 'Ard 'Eart, and recalled from retirement to the inner circle at the outbreak of war – asked for an urgent meeting with Fisher and Churchill.

The problem was that it was not clear from the signal alone where they would be heading, nor if they were going to be accompanied by the main fleet – Oliver decided probably not. If the target was a town on the English north east coast, then it could be anywhere from Newcastle to Harwich. What should be done? It did not seem to occur to either Wilson or Oliver that it might have been sensible to consult people from Room 40, or they would have found that other clues were available. Jellicoe was informed and wanted to take his whole fleet to sea. He was told that the intelligence did not justify it, and as a compromise he was told to send a squadron of his most modern battleships. So Beatty's battlecruisers set sail for Rosyth, with orders to rendezvous at Dogger Bank – midway between Scarborough and Heligoland Bight – supported by the Second Battle Squadron under Sir George Warrender.

Churchill was in his bath on the morning of 16 December when there was a knock on the door and the message was handed in. The German battlecruiser force was bombarding Hartlepool and other north east coast towns. He leapt out, and not stopping to dry himself, fumbled into his wet clothes, and dashed down to the chart room. Fisher had just arrived and Oliver, who slept by his desk, was already marking the ships onto the main charts.

"We went on tenterhooks to breakfast," wrote Churchill later. "To have this tremendous prize – the German battle squadron whose loss would fatally mutilate the whole German navy and could never be repaired – actually within our claws, and to have the event turn upon a veil of mist was a racking ordeal."

As it turned out, it would be a very close thing indeed, because Admiral Friedrich von Ingenohl was also at sea with the whole German High Seas Fleet, not far behind Hipper and operating the perennial German plan – to use the battlecruisers as bait to overwhelm a smaller British force. As it was, Friedrich von Ingenohl was having nerves. When he encountered the destroyers that were screening Warrender's squadron, in the early hours of 16 December, he was horrified – afraid he had fallen into a similar British trap, and turned his fleet around, abandoning Hipper's battlecruisers to their fate. Warrender must have been aware that he had encountered units of the whole enemy fleet but seems not to have reported it. Beatty could hear the guns and steered his battlecruisers towards it, and at one stage the three units – Warrender, Beatty and Hipper – were steaming towards each other at a combined speed of 40 knots. Then disappointment. An ambiguous signal sent by Beatty to his own scouting cruisers – Commodore William Goodenough in the *Southampton* – led to them breaking off contact and moving back to position ahead of the battlecruisers, a manoeuvre that was supposed to happen only when battle was about to be joined.

So Warrender escaped from the High Seas Fleet, and Hipper escaped from Beatty. Admiral Alfred von Tirpitz, the founder of the modern German navy, complained later that von Ingenohl had "the fate of Germany in the palm of his hand, I boil with inward emotion whenever I think of it." It is true that, if Warrender's battle squadron had been annihilated, it would have been the most extraordinary victory over the unbeatable British navy. And even with the secrets of Room 40, the British had not been able to corner Hipper, or avenge the men, women and children killed in Hartlepool. Worse, the basic problems of naval planning were now clear – and they were largely about information. The cryptographers had not been consulted. Vital information had not been passed on by commanders at sea, and the flag signals preferred by the British in the heat of battle had let them down again. There in a nutshell was the story of the war at sea. It was to happen again and again.

**

Early the next year, the moment they had all dreaded finally arrived. Room 40 found they could not read the signals. The SKM code had been changed at last, a mere four months after the codebook had been captured on board the *Magdeburg*. "Now the dreadful change had come!" wrote Denniston later. "All the available staff were summoned by telephone and, after a night long struggle, the new key was obtained to the joy and admiration of all concerned".

Actually, the code turned out not to have been changed after all. It transpired that the cipher had only been 'slid'. It was ciphered using exactly the same basis, and using the same key, just that the starting point had been shifted so that it appeared to be a new one. So when, on 23 January, it became clear that the battlecruisers were venturing out again, it was once again clear from the signal traffic. Fisher had a cold and was recuperating at home. His ancient deputy, Sir Arthur Wilson, came into Churchill's without knocking and announced: "Those fellows are coming out again".

Churchill and Wilson gathered their top decision-makers to decide what to do. Even then, no signal had been sent to prepare the Jellicoe and the Grand Fleet for sea. He was a good 140 miles away from the action, and was to complain later about delays in information, as well he might. But Oliver and Wilson were still operating in the old, pre-wireless, even pre-Dreadnought world, where decisions did not have to be made instantaneously. The Grand Fleet would need to get up steam. They would need to file out of the booms that protected Scapa Flow, before they could make their way south and twenty knots, and at vast expense, to intercept the enemy.

Beatty's battlecruisers were as far south as Rosyth, and could potentially reach the Yorkshire coast where the Hipper and the German battlecruisers were expected. Within hours, Beatty had steam up and soon his elegant ships, belching smoke, *Lion, Princess Royal, Tiger, Indomitable, New Zealand*, were speeding south. The first battlecruiser-on-battlecruiser action was about to take place.

Hipper was outgunned, with only three battlecruisers and the old heavy cruiser *Blücher*. On paper at least, Beatty had the advantage in guns on his side, but he did not have what any naval commander needs, however gallant: *luck*. The British signal system was archaic. In battle, British ships hoisted enormous 'battle ensigns' to prevent them from being mistaken for the other side, but the signal flags remained as small as ever, and easy to misinterpret in the heat of battle.

The two battlecruiser squadrons clashed at breakfast time on 24 January, with both sides received a battering as they ran south west towards the German home port. Beatty had no shortage of grit in battle but, once again, his supplies of luck were becoming scarce. His flagship *Lion* was damaged and began to fall behind the battle, just as his superior numbers were beginning to overwhelm Hipper's squadron. At this critical moment, this robbed Beatty of victory at Dogger Bank.

First, he received reports in U-boats in the vicinity and ordered his ships to turn away briefly from the battle. It was an unnecessary manoeuvre, not because torpedoes might not have been deadly for the battlecruisers, but because – in Whitehall, but excluded from decision-making – Hope knew where all the U-boats were, and had reported this to Oliver, but it had taken two hours to signal and reassure Beatty that none were anywhere near. By then, it was too late.

Second, there was a fatal confusion as *Lion*, wounded and listing over to starboard, disappeared into the distance. Beatty hoisted a signal to his second in command, Rear-Admiral Gordon Moore, urging him to attack the rear of the enemy. But the old signal about turning away to avoid submarines was also still flying, alongside the order for a turn-away course of north east. Moore interpreted this confusion as a direct order to concentrate on the struggling and crippled *Blücher*.

Beatty could see what was happening and tried to hoist Nelson's famous signal to "engage the enemy more closely" but it wasn't in the signal book. By the time the flag codes for "keep nearer to the enemy" had been hoisted, Lion was too far behind the battle for the signal to be visible. *Blücher* rolled over and sank, but the rest of Hipper's ships escaped to fight another day.

**

The spring of 1915 was emerging in St James's Park behind the Admiralty, as you could see through the windows of Room 40. The various fleet encounters had now sunk the careers of Warrender , Moore and von Ingenohl. Poison gas was used for the first time in April, the *Lusitania* was torpedoed and sunk in May. And Hall was getting into his stride as the malevolent genius of signal decrypts. His key objective, as director of naval intelligence, was somehow to lure the German High Seas Fleet out from its anchorage at Wilhelmshaven, so that it could be brought to action.

At his instigation, Churchill sent dummy battlecruisers – as well as a real one – to the Dardanelles, hoping that it might tempt Hipper out under the impression that Beatty's force was below strength. Together with Lt Col Reginald Drake, later head of G Branch at MI5, he faked a series of photos which appeared to show that Beatty's flagship *Lion* was taking much longer to repair after the Battle of Dogger Bank than had been expected. In doing so, he successfully lured away the U-boats which had been lying in wait for her first sea trial out of dry dock.

But Hall was not stopping there. The next stage was for he and Drake to send false reports back, using the names of spies who had actually been arrested – a technique that was perfected in the Second World War – to give the impression that they had uncovered military preparations to invade the German coast in Schleswig-Holstein. The purpose was to force the enemy fleet out to defend their coast. In fact, this rather backfired. The Germans believed the reports and their moves in response, shifting troops up towards the coast, were interpreted by British military intelligence as preparation for an invasion of Britain. The resulting counter-moves and mutual distrust made the German fleet if anything more defensive. Either way, it stayed put. It also convinced Hall's superiors, and Oliver in particular, that the German fleet intended to break out through the English Channel, which confused decision-making at a critical moment later on.

The Dardanelles campaign was also now taking up Hall's attention, and marked two of his most daring escapades. First, on his own initiative – and without reference to higher authority – he offered contacts inside the Turkish government £4 million to conclude a peace and allow the Anglo-French fleet free passage through the narrows and into Constantinople.

Hall described the encounter with his chiefs. "Who authorised this?" asked Churchill.

"I did, First Lord," said Hall.

"But – the cabinet surely knows nothing about it?"

"No, it does not. But if we were to get peace, or if we were to get a peaceful passage for that amount, I imagine they'd be glad enough to pay."

Fisher was still busy writing, and Churchill turned to him. "D'you hear what this man has done? He's told his people they can go up to four million to buy a peaceful passage! On his own!"

But Fisher was determined to send the fleet through and insisted that the negotiations were ended. The first attempt by the fleet to force the Dardanelles took place on 18 March with disastrous results: more ships were lost than at any time since Trafalgar. "Ironically," wrote Hall later, "when the gallant attempt of March 18 had been unsuccessful, the cabinet were asking me to spare no expense to win over the Turks. Unfortunately, it was then too late."

The Dardanelles led to Fisher's repeated resignations. By the end of their partnership, the Admiralty was virtually paralysed by their in-fighting and, after six months in the job, senior officers there were already regarding Hall as the most fearless fixer. They asked him to use his influence to sort it out.

He arranged to see the Lord Chief Justice, Lord Reading, at Herschell's flat and to set out the problems the Admiralty was facing – Reading actually lived two doors from Hall in Curzon Street. When he had finished, Reading cross-examined him for half an hour – he had been the famous barrister Rufus Isaacs – and asked him which of the two, Churchill or Fisher, should go. This is how Hall described the encounter later:

"It was the crucial question for which I had been waiting. 'Regretfully,' I told him, 'I have to say both.'

'And why?'

'Because if you wish, as you must, to maintain any confidence between the fleet and the Admiralty, you mustn't keep a First lord who will have appeared to have driven out of office a man like Lord Fisher The Navy would never forgive him.'

Lord Reading nodded and for a moment there was silence. 'You were quite right,' he said at last, 'when you said that you were putting your future in my hands, and if you had answered my questions differently I would have broken you. But I am now satisfied that your view of what is required is correct, and I will see the Prime Minister at once.'"

**

While Hall was taking it upon himself to re-arrange the leadership of the navy, and shuffle the cabinet, he was perfecting the art of the intelligence dirty trick. He created his own fake code book, to be used only at a time of national crisis – called the Secret Emergency War Code – and had it sold to the Germans by a representative in Rotterdam for £500. He even took it upon himself, after the disaster of the Battle of the Somme in 1916, when some kind of diversion was required, to intervene on the Western Front. He sent out a series of messages in a simple, crackable code that implied some kind of Belgian invasion by the allies, in order to relieve the troops opposite the battered British forces further south.

It was never clear if this was a plan carried out without the involvement of the War Office, but it probably was done with their knowledge. Hall was a loose cannon, but he was a highly responsible one and he believed strongly in getting on with people in other departments, and he quickly healed the rift with the army which had been caused by kicking them out of the Hunstanton Lifeboat Station. He may have been ruthless, but he was also charming and loyal to his friends and his staff – and very aware that he needed influence in a range of other circles in British life, hence his recruitment of assistants who understood other social circles.

In fact, when Admiral Godfrey took up the same job in 1939, he asked Hall for his advice, and good quality assistants with links to other areas of public life was high on his list. It was the main reason why Godfrey recruited Ian Fleming, the creator of the fictional spy James Bond. Hall's influence is clear, though indirect, on the creation of Bond's world.

Though Hall still had no direct control over it, it was also clear that Room 40 needed a great deal more cryptographers. The signals they could read were getting more numerous, and the kinds of traffic they were aspiring to tackle were getting wider. It was at this point, when Hall was still not in complete charge, with Ewing still hanging on as nominal leader, that Room 40 forged the beginning of a long-term link between King's College, Cambridge – a link that would eventually lead to the recruitment of Alan Turing nearly a quarter of a century later.

Dillwyn Knox was the fellow of King's and an expert on ancient Greek papyrus documents. His recruitment marked a recognition by Ewing that the academic rigour of reconstructing ancient texts might be relevant to reconstructing modern signals in code. This was an important element of the British approach to cryptography, in both world wars: the recognition that a wide variety of skills and knowledge was more important than a very specific kind of expertise.

Knox was, by some way, the most important of the wartime recruits and it was the beginning for him of a lifetime in naval code-breaking. He was given Room 53, next door to Room 40, as his own office and it happened to have a bath fitted. He used to spend all night there, mulling in the warm water until morning, while his notes got covered in soap. Then there would be a flurry of activity before his secretary arrived. This intimacy with Olive Roddam, this wartime assistant, was unusual for a bachelor fellow, and Knox was soon in love. The two married at the end of 1917. When he was out of the bath, Knox still looked like an academic. He had been given a naval uniform, in line with his position, but it was said that it "hung on him like a sack".

Frank Birch was also a fellow of King's and a historian. But he had served in the RNVR (Royal Naval Volunteer Reserve) in the Dardanelles, so – unlike most of those in Room 40 – he had some naval experience. He was also destined to spend most of the rest of his career in naval cryptography. He also married during the war and he and Knox tried to live in the same house in Chelsea, before the Knoxes decamped to High Wycombe.

Some of the new recruits came directly under Hall, bypassing Ewing's control of Room 40. The Rev William Montgomery came from Westminster Presbyterian College in Cambridge, and an expert on St Augustine. Knox's brother provided something of a balance, since he was now Fr Ronald Knox, a prominent Catholic convert, who could be seen around Room 40 from time to time in his long black, clerical robes.

Other recruits came because Hall wanted better contacts in some of the areas of public life that he was not familiar with. Lord Herschell became his assistant to give him access to court circles. The stockbroker Claud Serocold helped him to cover the City of London. The publisher Nigel de Grey had failed his diplomatic exams because his Italian was hardly up to scratch, but he arrived to give access to publishing circles. Unusually for Room 40, de Grey had seen active service, in this case in the Royal Naval Balloon Section.

These were all enthusiastic amateurs when it came to codebreaking. Their skill was not in mathematics and they were certainly not code specialists, but they all brought a kind of logic to the task, an ability to recognise patterns and reconstruct documents, which had been Dilly Knox's expertise at King's. By close attention to patterns, Knox was able to reconstruct a Hungarian codebook without knowing any Hungarian, an extraordinary feat, even for a logician.

It was Knox in 1917 who was responsible for the most famous leap of logical imagination of the war, the spark of genius that unlocked the new German flag officer's code which had replaced the VB codebook, known as VB, which had originally emerged in the 'miraculous draught of fishes'. He noticed that one early message seemed to repeat the same two letters at the ends of lines, -en. What kind of discourse repeated the same two letters over and over again? Could it possibly be a poem of some kind?

Recognising a poem in German was a task for a specialist and Knox took it to Leonard Willoughby, who suggested a poem by Schiller. It fitted. It was the breakthrough to tackling the code that was being used to control the U-boats, and not a moment too soon since they had been unleashed with deadly force against allied shipping from the start of 1917. By the middle of the year, the whole codebook had been reconstructed.

Chapter 4
Jutland

"There can be few purely mental experiences more charged with cold excitement than to follow, almost from minute to minute, the phases of a great naval action from the silent rooms of the Admiralty, out on blue water in the fighting ships, amid the stunning detonation of the cannonade, fractions of the event unfold themselves to the corporeal eye, there is the sense of action at its highest: there is the wrath of battle; there is the intense, self-effecting physical or mental toil. But in Whitehall only the clock ticks and quiet men enter with quick steps, laying slips of pencilled paper before other men equally silent who draw lines, scribble calculations, and point with the definer or make brief subdued comments."

So Winston Churchill described the experience of a naval battle from the chart room of the Admiralty, aware of the clamour of sea and smoke from moment to moment, but so far away. It was also the experience the navy longed for once war had been declared. The stakes were so high. A great fleet action, by the two greatest ironclad fleets in history, would be either another Trafalgar or – could it even be spoken? It was Churchill himself who described Sir John Jellicoe, the commander-in-chief, as "the only man who could lose the war in an afternoon".

If the Western Front had been an unexpected stalemate and a new kind of war, then the war at sea was becoming much the same. The whole Admiralty, both the amateur team of cryptographers and the crusty old sea dogs who held them in contempt, longed for the great clash. But major confrontations at sea were becoming increasingly rare. The early years of the war was studded with moments of overwhelming excitement and high hopes, ordering the Grand Fleet so laboriously and expensively to sea, only to sweep pointlessly across the North Sea and home again at dusk disappointed and frustrated. Appalling as the bombarding of Scarborough, Hartlepool or Whitby from the sea had been, at least it had provided an opportunity for a knock-out naval victory.

Room 40 was now able to give advance warning of a sortie, but the German Navy was finally understanding their vulnerability when it came to wireless signalling. They were now changing the ciphers once a month, and the night duty team at Room 40 were expected to crack it by dawn. This was not always as difficult as it sounded, at least by the middle of the war, because the new cipher key was usually announced by wireless and often started before the new books could be distributed to the ships, so signals were often reciphered using the old key, which made them easy to translate and gave a complete guide to the new one.

Early in 1916, the German navy changed their HVB code with a new one known as AFB (*Allgemeinefunkspruchbuch*), used mainly for communicating with U-boats and zeppelins. At the same time, a new commander-in-chief was appointed to the High Seas Fleet, and Admiral Reinhard Scheer was determined to make things happen. It was soon clear that something was going on.

**

The basic German plan had barely changed. It was to lure out part of the Grand Fleet on a trajectory which took them over an arc of concentrated U-boats and then to overwhelm them with the whole High Seas Fleet. Scheer's version of the plan depended on surprise and then overwhelming force.

Room 40 realised that something was up when the German submarines were ordered to sea on 16 May and then failed to appear in their usual positions on the trade routes. But the first definite evidence of plans came a fortnight later, on 30 May, just after 10am. This was another signal to the submarines, warning them that their own forces would be at sea from 31 May to 1 June. They must, at all costs, avoid friendly torpedoes. What was happening?

Here the over-secretive arrangements which had been put in place by Churchill and Fisher began to work the wrong way. Sir Henry Oliver, as the First Sea Lord's chief assistant, was still treating signals intelligence as if it was his private conduit of information, and as if it was up to him alone to assess it and to dispose the fleet accordingly. And Oliver, as it happened, was obsessed with the idea that the German fleet were planning an attack on the English Channel.

This may have been partly the fault of Blinker Hall, whose dirty tricks operations had focused on coastal attacks for years in order to lure the High Seas Fleet out of port. But equally, Oliver seems not to have felt the need to consult the cryptographers about the interpretation of their signals, and at this stage Room 40 had already identified all the enemy ships that would be involved. Just before noon, the Admiralty's director of operations, Captain Thomas Jackson, the director of the operations division, came to see them. It was a rare event. In fact he had only come twice before, once to complain that he had cut himself on one of their red boxes and once to congratulate them that they weren't bothering with nonsense. He asked what the call sign DK meant. When he had been told, he left.

This was to have far-reaching consequences. Oliver and his operations team did not understand the significance of the signals information that was now available to Room 40. The importance of the DK signal was that it was Scheer's habitual subterfuge to transfer it to a shore establishment when he was at sea. Jackson was particularly dismissive of the efforts of Room 40, and despite his visit still had not understood what DK implied: that the flagship was at sea. Consequently, he and his colleagues were still unsure where the blow was going to fall, though both Beatty's battlecruisers and Jellicoe's main fleet had now been ordered to sea at 5.30pm on 30 May and were now belching smoke as they steamed south west through the night. And so it was that Oliver sent the fatal signal at 12.30pm on 31 May:

"No definite news of enemy. They made all preparations for sailing early this morning. It was thought fleet had sailed but directionals place flagship in Jade at 11.10am GMT. Apparently they have been unable to carry out air reconnaissance which has delayed them."

The cryptographers were furious when they discovered this piece of misinformation had been sent. It meant that Jellicoe slowed his squadrons down to conserve fuel. It meant that there would only be an hour of daylight left once the two fleets finally met. In short, it all but guaranteed Scheer's escape. It also fatally undermined confidence by the commanders at sea in the intelligence they were being given. "What am I to think of OD (Operations Division) when I get that telegram and, in three hours time, meet the whole German fleet well out at sea?"

Because the die was now cast. Hipper's five battlecruisers were steaming towards them, followed by the might of the High Seas Fleet. The two fleets were converging at the rate of about 40 miles an hour. The long-expected day was at hand.

It was not until 2.20 in the afternoon that Beatty's and Hipper's battlecruisers exchanged fire. It was Hipper's appointed task to turn round and draw Beatty's six battlecruisers, and the fast squadron of battleships not far behind, into the broadsides of the High Seas Fleet. Beatty had been lulled into a false sense of security by Oliver's fatal signal two hours before. His task was to destroy the enemy's ships. But, although he was respected across the navy as a dashing, fighting admiral, Beatty was once again no longer a lucky one. His luck had run short at Dogger Bank the previous year and it was now running low again. The fatal design flaws of the lightly armoured British battlecruisers were suddenly to be revealed.

Just after 4pm, his rear ship *Indefatigable* exploded in a ball of flame. Only 25 minutes later,

Queen Mary – Blinker Hall's old command – was blown sky high in the same way in a terrifying plume of smoke, appearing to collapse inwards. Beatty on the bridge of the *Lion*, which had only been saved from the same fate by an order from a dying marine major, turned to his flag captain and said: "There seems to be something wrong with our bloody ships today."

The battle had been going for only an hour when, out of the mist before them, Beatty, Commodore Goodenough in *Southampton* ahead of Beatty, watched to his astonishment as vanguard of the High Seas Fleet emerged into full view, stretching into the distance. Beatty's task was now clear. He must turn around and lead Scheer into the arms of Jellicoe's battleships, steaming full speed towards them.

**

The fundamental problem was also now clearer. What was developing, as they knew very well in London, was the biggest fleet action in history. Within hours, as Room 40 knew very well, the war could be won or lost. The signals were pouring in, being decoded and sent upstairs. What was also emerging was a clash between cultures. Nelson's victories had been with fleets small enough to control with flag signals. Jellicoe's fleet was so enormous and complex, and the distances were so huge, and the speeds so unprecedented, that something more was required. He needed information and, now that the crisis had arrived, he wasn't getting it. Neither was the rest of his fleet. "Where is enemy battlefleet?" he signalled to Beatty.

Jellicoe needed to know precisely where the enemy fleet was because by far his most important decision was which way to get his battleships to deploy. Go one way and they would have an immediate disadvantage but would then leave the enemy in gloom while the dying sun silhouetted his own fleet as perfect targets. Go the other way, and the position would be reversed. But that was assuming he knew where the fleet was. He paced up and down on the metal deck of the admiral's bridge on Iron Duke. Everyone was silent. Then he gave the order quietly to deploy eastwards at 6.15pm.

It was the correct decision. The Grand Fleet deployed perfectly across the front of the enemy, able to fire on both sides simultaneously. It was a successful manoeuvre called 'Crossing the T' and it had been achieved perfectly. Jellicoe gave the order to open fire at 6.30pm. As soon as he realised what was happening, Scheer gave the order to the German fleet to turn away, each ship in its place turning 180 degrees. It was another manoeuvre achieved with perfection, and done behind a screen of smoke and a torpedo attack by destroyers.

Scheer turned back, steering north east to get to the east of the British, but Jellicoe anticipated him and once more crossed the German T at 7pm. This time, Scheer ordered Hipper and the battered battlecruisers into a suicidal attack, with the destroyers, to cover the escape of the fleet. This time, Jellicoe made what turned out to be his own fatal decision, to turn away to avoid the torpedoes, and contact was lost.

Jellicoe contented himself that his huge fleet was still sailing between the German Fleet and their base, but the previous few hours had flagged up a number of problems that would be important. First, there was clearly a problem about the capacity of British shells to explode at some angles. This was to be tackled immediately after the battle. Second, the protection of the British battlecruisers appeared to be inadequate when they were used in these fleet actions. There was little that could be done about that in the short-term. But the third problem went to the heart of the Room 40 problem: Jellicoe faced a serious lack of information. His own captains failed to keep him informed and, although the code information was piling up at the Admiralty, it was not being understood or passed on.

This was particularly a problem when it came to working out where Scheer would go next. Jellicoe assumed he would be making for the Ems, due south. Actually, he was making for Horns Reef. He would not be making the same route as Jellicoe was imagining. At 7.40pm, Scheer ordered his destroyers to attack the British fleet with torpedoes during the night. It was decoded and passed to Oliver, but it took an hour and 25 minutes to pass it on to the flagship at sea. Detailed instructions were also decoded and were not passed on at all. At 9.55pm, Room 40 decoded orders to Scheer that included a course and speed. This was passed to Jellicoe but without any emphasis on how reliable this intelligence was. By then he was frustrated and disillusioned with the information he was receiving and he discounted it.

Fifteen minutes later, came the clincher. The order was decoded sending zeppelins over Horns Reef for reconnaissance. It was never passed to Jellicoe. In fact, at this stage, Oliver was beside his desk taking a nap, well-deserved, but he had not left instructions that he should be woken if coded signals came through. Nor did he read back over the previous decodes when he did wake. During night, the sixteen German signals were decoded that included information about the direction and position of the fleet, but only three were passed on to Jellicoe, and they were sent without interpretation or explanation. Even if he had been sent the information about where the High Seas Fleet was by 1.15am, he still could have caught some of them.

Worse, for Jellicoe, his own captains failed to keep him informed either. What was actually happening was that Scheer's fleet was creeping through the destroyer screen to Jellicoe's rear and using its superior night-fighting abilities to good effect. A series of encounters had been heard by most of Jellicoe's fleet, but his captains assumed he must also have heard the explosions – and Jellicoe assumed it must relate to the decrypt he had received about destroyer attacks. Five British destroyers were now at the bottom of the North Sea, and they had torpedoed and sunk two German cruisers and the old battleship *Pommern.* Nobody reported the encounters in any detail and with any authority to the flagship. When Jellicoe and his commanders woke next morning, ready for action, the North Sea was empty.

It was one of the greatest disappointments for the navy of the whole war. The battle had ended with the exit of one side, having inflicted serious damage on the other, and before the great clash could have reached a crescendo. It also guaranteed the continuation of the war. If Jellicoe had been able to fulfil the purpose of his appointment, when he had taken over the fleet on Fisher's orders on the outbreak of war, and had destroyed their German opponents, it is tempting to imagine that history would have been very different. It is too easy to blame Oliver for trying to oversee the entire battle himself. Every one of the 148 orders sent to naval units during the battle from the Admiralty were drafted by him. The significance of the signal information, and the depth of the information they revealed, was not understood by Oliver or his colleagues because hardly any of them knew about Room 40 – and those that did know something tended to be biased against the whole idea. Jellicoe did not know where the information was coming from, because no conclusions were drawn from it, and because he not been told the source. A generation later, Hall's Second World War successor John Godfrey solved the problem partly by introducing a grading system. He need not say that the information came from Enigma, but he could say that it was certain. Nothing like that was available to Jellicoe, who bore the brunt of the blame – and at that stage few naval thinkers had realised the problem of information faced by huge hierarchical organisations, needing to take complex and immediate decisions.

Perhaps Jellicoe should have anticipated that problem, as he anticipated so much else. He certainly deserves some of the blame that not one report reached him that the German fleet was slipping through his own destroyer screen to escape. But the real blame must lie with Churchill's original system for dealing with the decrypts – constructed before the significance of what was happening had become clear. It was hugely centralised and far too secretive. It allowed none of the connections to be made. It allowed huge expertise to be built up in a corner of the Admiralty, which was derided by senior officers who should have known better, but simply never explained to anyone else.

The Grand Fleet was, in some ways, the blueprint for the twentieth century phenomenon: the giant hierarchical corporation and, as we were to discover later, these had huge difficulties getting information to decision-makers and spreading it down to the complex tentacles. It was a system that threatened to grind to a halt through lack of information: Jutland was the moment that very twentieth century problem became clear – if anyone was listening.

But Blinker Hall was paying attention. It was largely because of Hall that a system emerged that was capable of putting the information to use, and – because of his influence – some systematic solutions were used in the Second World War. But the ultimate indignity was still to come, as a bitter Jellicoe and battered Beatty made their way back to their respective anchorages. The German news agency got their version of the battle out first, so the first communiqué that reached Edinburgh was about a British defeat. It was said that the sailors returning to Rosyth were booed in Princes Street.

**

Jutland had been the biggest clash between fleets in history – at least before the age of the aircraft carrier made direct clashes rare. It remains so, in that sense, to this day. It was also, at least for the British, a massive disappointment. The battle might not have happened at all if it had not been for the Room 40 cryptographers, but with Churchill and Fisher's arrangements and Oliver's proprietary control over Room 40, the opportunity to end the war with a titanic naval battle had been missed.

Jellicoe complained after Jutland. Balfour, Churchill's successor, assured him that he had received the best intelligence they had. It was not true. He had been initiated into the Room 40 secret, but only in the broadest terms and had hoped to organise decrypts in his own flagship. In practice, Jellicoe only had another six months as commander-in-chief. He would come to the Admiralty himself as First Sea Lord in November and was succeeded at Scapa Flow by Beatty, while the rival supporters of both men fought the great behind-the-scenes battle over who was responsible for the great disappointment of Jutland.

That opportunity was never to come again. Jellicoe's period at the Admiralty was dominated by the controversy about convoys and whether they were the best way of dealing with the U-boat menace. But change was in the air. Blinker Hall was finally bringing his influence and his plans to fruition, and there was no more capable operator in the navy.

Just before Jutland, Ewing had been offered the job of principal of Edinburgh University. Balfour didn't encourage him to stay, though he clearly would have been liked to have been asked. In fact, Ewing was never thanked for his pioneering work by the Admiralty. Oliver tried to get him the OBE but it was turned down. The exact reason for this is not quite clear, but it might be possible to detect the subtle influence of Hall behind the official disenchantment with Ewing. Either way, Hall inherited Room 40.

The problem was still far from being solved. Room 40 still not integrated with the intelligence division, and the excessive secrecy, that kept the knowledge gleaned from reading the enemy's signals from being used, was still in place. Most of what an intelligence service ought to be doing was not, in fact, codified at all, and that suited Hall very well. He was charming and effective, but he liked to keep his hands close to his chest. It remains one reason why definitive knowledge about intelligence in the First World War remains so scarce.

His first move was to enlarge the staff again. It was at this point that Fr Ronald Knox joined the cryptographers, as well as the author Desmond McCarthy , the music critic Francis Toye and a few actors. He also employed women, including the cigar-smoking Lady Hambro and Olive Reddam, who was to marry Dilly Knox. Hall charmed his staff and they would do anything for him. "My car is outside," he used to say to them, at appropriate moments. "Go out for a breath of air!" He also got them uniforms to go with their commissions, though they tended to forget their caps. One member of the team used to wear his back to front, to the consternation of regular officers.

Hope had become the effective executive officer of Room 40 and he took this opportunity to escape back to sea, where he took command of the cruiser *Dartmouth*. With great difficulty, Hall managed to extract Commander William James, who had been his second-in-command on *Queen Mary*. James had the nickname 'Bubbles', because it was well known in the navy that he had been, as a curly-haired child, the original for the famous Millais painting of the boy blowing soap bubbles, which was used eventually for advertising Pears Soap. James was a high-flyer, and was Hall's eventual biographer, and was more of a conventional naval officer than Hope. But he was also effective at healing the breach between Room 40 and the senior staff officers.

By May 1917, Room 40 had been integrated into the intelligence division, and there was another important breakthrough. Paymaster Commander Ernest Thring had been plotting the position of U-boats using other available intelligence, a job he would take on for a second time in 1939, and he was finally let in on the great secret and given the decrypts which could help him. Six months later, with the U-boat threat becoming intense, Jellicoe formed the Anti-submarine Division at the Admiralty, and its chief was allowed to see the decrypts too.

Chapter 5
Zimmerman

Hall's next task was to heal the rift with the military cryptographers. MI1(b) had been developed under a new broom, Captain Malcolm Hay, who had been shot in the face in the first few weeks of the war and was eventually swapped as a prisoner of war on the Dutch frontier and brought home. When he arrived at the War Office, he found one code-breaker, Oliver Strachey – brother of the more famous Lytton – engaged in wrestling with diplomatic signals.

It was Hay and Strachey who worked out how they might get hold of the American diplomatic code. This involved sending them a proposal in plain text from the Foreign Office – who had quite reasonably to be kept in the dark as well – knowing that the text would then be encrypted before it was sent out to Washington. They would then have the perfect key. If Hall's operation at the Admiralty came to dominate the business of listening in to neutral or enemy diplomatic signals, then it began at MI1(b).

But the two sides were still nursing the wounds which began when the War Office had been kicked out of Hunstanton Lifeboat Station. It was Hall's task to heal the rift, or at least to begin to. He and Hay built up a close relationship, which could not actually blossom until Hall had managed to ease out Ewing and take full control of Room 40 himself. But their mutual regard and reliance on each other was so strong before Hall's small coup, that – when MI1(b) moved to Cork Street, Piccadilly – Hay had a private telephone link installed direct to Hall. It became a kind of intelligence hotline.

The fact that they were co-operating on signal interception at all was because, from 1915, they were both listening in to diplomatic messages. Hall's assistant George Young suggested a diplomatic cryptographic section and Hall leapt at the idea, forming it outside Ewing's control.

Hall was already concerned about other letters leaving the country. Like Fisher, Hall would talk to anyone – and he surrounded himself with people who could were able to talk to people in most areas of public life. It was a conversation he had with a lowly censor clerk which convinced him that letters from businesses from neutral countries, but based in the UK, might include information about where Germany was trying to buy food or raw materials in foreign markets. He went to see Colonel George

Cockerill at MI5 and persuaded him that all the mail should be opened before it left the country.

The problem turned out to be that the mail censorship department of the War Office was beginning to break down under the strain. Hall offered to come up with a better scheme, and – walking backwards and forwards between the Admiralty and his flat in Mayfair – he came up with one. Four days later, it was up and running, staffed by members of the National Service League. The Home Secretary demanded to see him, and accused him of interfering with the mail. By the end of the interview, the ministers had been mollified and the War Trade Intelligence Department had been born.

**

Perhaps the nation had never needed intelligence on the scale that it did now. Perhaps nobody with Hall's peculiar combination of charm, energy, devious secrecy and sheer ambition, had ever held a senior intelligence role before. But in a few years, he had set a pattern. There was no jape, not scheme, he would not turn his mind to. He was happy to bribe and double cross where necessary, along the lines which became famously successful in the Second World War. Most of his schemes were never written down, most perhaps not remembered at all, and those which were remembered were packaged as

Hall wanted them remembered. There was no area of the war effort, no part of the globe, that he considered outside his remit.

It was Hall who bribed an Anglo-German in Belgium to copy a military code book page by page. It was almost certainly Hall who had him shot when he lost his nerve. It was Hall who sold a fake edition of the British Naval Emergency War Code – as he called it – to the enemy. It was Hall who strong-armed South American cable offices to hand over the texts of German cables. It was Hall who recruited the novelist A. E. W. Mason, author of *Fire Over England*, to sail the Caribbean in his yacht and to bring about the destruction of a clandestine German radio station in Mexico. When he uncovered a plot to infect Argentine beef with anthrax, or when anthrax spores were sent in a German diplomatic bag to attack reindeer in the far north, it was Hall who warned the Norwegians, and who seized the bags and discovered the plot.

Any one of these little schemes would make a book in themselves, but the key wheeze here – which led to such far-reaching consequences – was what happened in 1916 when the Romanian government declared war on Germany. It came to Hall's attention that the gardener at the German embassy in Bucharest had seen the military attaché burying something in the garden. Inside was evidence of a plot for germ warfare. All in a day's work for the director of naval intelligence.

**

The story goes that the German Foreign Under-Secretary Arthur Zimmermann had a pet plan to set the middle east alight, rather as Lawrence of Arabia on behalf of the British. His chosen instrument was an intelligence officer called Wilhelm Wassmuss, who was – like Lawrence – something of a loner, steeped in Arab culture and difficult to get on with. It was his task to wander incognito and to stir up a Muslim *jihad* against the British and French.

Like Lawrence, Wassmuss was hardly easy to control. He fell out with his colleagues and travelled to Persia, where he started his own guerrilla war. Also like Lawrence, he was briefly captured but not recognised, this time by the British in Bushire early in 1915. But if Wassmuss escaped, his two companions did not, and neither did his luggage. It was opened, found to contain propaganda designed to stir up some kind of revolt against British rule in India, sent to the India Office in London and forgotten.

That much was true. But Hall admitted later that he had made up the story of what happened next to cover up the truth, which was much more complicated but remains hidden. He is supposed to have heard about Wassmuss's luggage from a junior intelligence officer, sent round for it from the India Office, opened it and found the codebook for the German diplomatic code known as 13040.

This is not true, but the codes he did find in the luggage came at the time George Young had suggested setting up a diplomatic division under Hall, and they definitely provided the basis for decryption and analysis of the German diplomatic traffic from then on. Young set up in Room 45, with a copy of the VB code book and the contents of Wassmuss's luggage. It was possible to intercept German diplomatic cables because, since the Atlantic cables had been cut, all cables to the Americas needed to be routed via the UK. Often they were sent via the Swedish embassy where they were supposed to have diplomatic immunity, a source of continuing friction with the Swedes.

But if it is not clear how Hall cracked the 13040 code, whether from Wassmuss or from some other skulduggery, it came to have enormous significance early in 1917, when it led to the interception of decryption of the famous Zimmerman Telegram.

**

To understand the background to the most momentous telegram ever sent, we have to go back to July 1916. Jutland has just been fought, the

British and their allies are dying in unprecedented numbers on the Somme, and the American general John Pershing is fighting in Mexico in pursuit of Pancho Villa. It isn't going well for him.

The Germans were also watching closely. Room 45 decrypted a German diplomatic signal from their ambassador in Washington. "It becomes clearer and clearer that the American government has drawn back from a rupture because her military resources are not sufficient to face a war with Mexico." This was an example of the kind of wishful thinking that characterises so much of wartime diplomacy. The German government was beginning to conclude that the USA was even more reluctant to fight them than it seemed at the time, with President Woodrow Wilson desperately trying to broker some kind of ceasefire between the warring nations, but being drawn inexorably towards war.

In November, the war came a little closer. German Foreign Minister, Gottlieb von Jagow, was sacked. He was an opponent of unrestricted submarine warfare, partly because it seemed incompatible with peaceful relations with the USA. Yet unleashing the U-boats without restraint now seemed to be one of the only paths open to them if they wanted any kind of negotiated settlement. Zimmermann took over, and he had a plan to keep the USA out.

It involved a tri-partite Pacific alliance between Germany, Mexico and Japan. Japan was nominally in the war already on the British side, but might – or so Zimmermann believed – be amenable to swap in return for progress in the emerging Japanese rivalry with the USA. Mexico was already all but at war with the USA, and perhaps might be persuaded to fight, in return for a promise that Germany would guarantee some of the territory lost to the USA back in the 1840s.

It was a bold idea, and there were few diplomatic options open to them. The Mexican ambassador to Berlin was away, so the original plan was to guarantee the secrecy of the plan by delivering the proposal to the Mexican government via a submarine. But given that they were planning to re-open unrestricted submarine warfare, that seemed perhaps to be asking for trouble, especially as the message was originally written to the German embassy in Washington.

As it was, the message was a long one. The text of the proposal was coded using the new 7500 code, but that was embedded into a longer message using the 13040 code, which included instructions. Cheekily, it was given to the US embassy in Berlin at 3pm on 16 January 1917, to transmit on, explaining that it was about Wilson's latest peace proposals.

The US embassy was happy to transmit it to the American legation in Copenhagen, which sent it on to the US embassy in London, which forwarded it to the State Department in Washington. The State Department objected in principle to passing on a long coded telegram when they had no idea what was in it. The president had to give his authority, and Wilson did. So it was not until 19 January that the message finally arrived at the German embassy in Washington, which passed it on to their embassy in Mexico City. All copies of the message at Germany's Washington embassy were burned: diplomats knew that an announcement about unrestricted submarine warfare was following soon, and they feared a final rift.

A copy of the signal was intercepted in London on the way out of the US embassy and it had arrived in Room 40, where – since Hall's coup – all messages now arrived, in the early hours of 17 January, while the original message was still delayed at the State Department. Those in charge of the night shift in that section were Dilly Knox and Nigel de Grey.

Knox looked first and filled in the bits he could read, and it was immediately clear that this looked important. De Grey had better German so he passed it over to him. By midday on 17 January, the basic text was clear, though 7500 was not a code they had mastered and parts were seriously incomplete. There was enough there for de Grey to realise he was looking at something explosive, enough to make him run next door to Hall's own office.

Hall was there, talking to Serocold. "Do you want America in the war, Sir?" he said quickly.

"Yes, why?"

"I've got a telegram that will bring them in if you give it to them."

There was then one of those moments that would become familiar in the next few weeks. Hall knew no German and he had to understand the significance with a barely readable text. "Blinker was no sort of fool," wrote de Grey later. "But he was patient with me and was convinced."

Hall locked the half-decoded message in the safe and swore the three of them to secrecy. This is what the telegram for Mexico said:

"We intend to begin on the first of February unrestricted submarine warfare. We shall endeavour in spite of this to keep the United States of America neutral. In the event of this not succeeding, we make Mexico a proposal of alliance on the following basis: make war together, make peace together, generous financial support and an understanding on our part that Mexico is to reconquer the lost territory in Texas, New Mexico, and Arizona. The settlement in detail is left to you. You will inform the President of the above most secretly as soon as the outbreak of war with the United States of America is certain and add the suggestion that he should, on his own initiative, invite Japan to immediate adherence and at the same time mediate between Japan and ourselves. Please call the President's attention to the fact that the ruthless employment of our submarines now offers the prospect of compelling England in a few months to make peace." Signed, ZIMMERMANN"

What could they do? The first task was to convince the Americans that the telegram was real, and without revealing where it came from – they could hardly explain that they were listening in to American diplomatic traffic. Yet how could they convince them without saying where they found the text? There needed to be a convincing cover story.

Hall puzzled this out in the following days. The telegram must have been transmitted on to Mexico City, he reasoned, and there was almost certainly a copy in the Western Union office. He remembered a mysterious figure, known to history as Mr H, who had just rescued a British national from a charge of forgery – and who happened to work in the telegraph office. By 10 February, Hall had a copy in his hands and his cover story was ready.

He also knew there needed to be an eminently believable emissary. Hall and de Grey concluded that the only British minister the Americans would trust was Balfour, now Foreign Secretary. Also, the time had to be right – and the USA might after all declare war once the unrestricted submarine warfare had begun. They had to wait.

On 5 February, there had been another message from Berlin, this time sent via the Swedish route – the Swedish 'roundabout' as they knew it in Room 40. It instructed the German ambassador to go ahead and propose the alliance to the Mexican president. Five days later, both messages had finally been decrypted by Room 40 in their entirety. It was also now clear that unrestricted submarine warfare was not, after all, going to push Wilson to declare war.

Hall decided it was time to act. He told his contact at the American embassy, the attaché Edward Bell, in strictest confidence, and asked him to say nothing until Balfour had decided what to do. The next day was 20 February and Balfour and a handful of trusted officials met Hall and decoded the telegram together. It was resolved that Balfour would hand a copy to the American ambassador, Walter Page, and that Hall would make the arrangements. "I think Captain Hall may be left to clinch this problem," said Balfour at the end of the meeting. "He knows the ropes better than anyone."

Three days later, it was in the hands of Page, but key American officials were away at the time, and it was not until 27 February that they finally decided what to do with it. By then rumours had begun to reach the British ambassador in Washington who cabled urgent requests for more information. Hall replied: "Premature exposure fatal," adding immodestly, "alone I did it."

Page was on borrowed time. He had fallen out with Wilson, his old friend, over their conflicting attitudes to the war. He had offered his resignation and, in fact, Wilson was already sounding out replacements. He knew the explosion the telegram would make in Washington, where pressure was also being brought to bear on Western Union there to disgorge a copy of the original from there. Hall spent the three days after the first meeting with Page, having staked everything on his plan, "in a kind of nightmare". So much could go wrong.

The news was released to the American press on 28 February and, as expected, there was absolute pandemonium, a mixture of outrage and serious doubts about the authenticity of the message. The press magnate William Randolph Hearst instructed his papers to treat the telegram like a forgery. But two days later, Zimmermann ended the speculation himself. Hearst's representative in Berlin begged him not to, but he decided on honesty. "I cannot deny it," he said. "It is true."

Wilson still hoped to avoid war, but the revelation that the Germans were planning to subdivide the union, and had sent a coded message proposing it using American diplomatic channels, was too powerful a fact to overcome. On 20 March, his cabinet voted unanimously for war. Congress followed suit on 2 April and the rest was history.

**

The entry of the USA into the war on the allied side came immediately before the great crisis in the Atlantic. In April 1917 alone, nearly a million tons of shipping was sunk by U-boats, and more than half of that was British. Food queues began to frighten the government. There were reports of people in Sheffield eating raw horsemeat, seasoned by salt. The first major push to grow food on allotments on marginal land around the cities was under way, and was eventually a huge success.

In May, Room 40 was finally integrated into the Naval Intelligence Division under Hall officially, rather than just in reality. It was then that Paymaster-Commander Thring, whose task it was to track the U-boats, was finally given access to the decrypted intelligence. The battle over whether to introduce convoys, as they had in the Napoleonic War, was being waged with bitter ferocity in the Admiralty. But when it was introduced, in May 1917, it was immediately obvious that it was a good idea. From June onwards, the U-boats failed to reach their target of 600,000 tons sunk a month.

Now that it had some kind of official legitimacy, Hall could expand Room 40 nearly as fast as he wanted. By Spring 1918, when the allies were being pushed back by the sudden success of the Ludendorf Offensive on the Western Front, there were 74 male cryptographers and 33 female, with assorted support staff, and they had long since burst out of the confines of Room 40 itself. By then, the Germans had set up their own decryption centre *Entzifferungsdienst* or E-dienst, based at Neumünster. Between Kiel and Hamburg, it was too far away either from the fleet command at Wilhelmshaven or the Admiralty in Berlin, but it was able to make the fleet more aware how vulnerable their signal codes had become.

Towards the end of October 1918, there were once again signs in the signals that the German High Seas Fleet was preparing a final do-or-die sortie into the North Sea. It was delayed on 30 October and cancelled the following day. Then on 1 November, the first hints began to appear that something was going on in the German fleet. On 5 November, there was a signal ordering commanders to lock away al signal codes. Bitterly frustrated to have mouldered away in harbour for two years, as their food rations and those of their families were cut and cut, there was a mutiny under way among the crews of the German navy. Hall was still energetic, faking photographs of naval mutinies in the UK to encourage the German mutineers.

The final events of the First World War are beyond the scope of this book. But when Beatty led the Grand Fleet to sea to meet their defeated enemy, ten days after the armistice, it was still not clear whether the encounter would be peaceful. It was a misty day in the North Sea as the battleships waited for the encounter and a tense moment. The ships were cleared for action and it was widely believed that, when the moment came, the German battleships would not in fact surrender.

As they came into sight, steaming in a long grey line, they were sighted on the new battleship HMS *Royal Oak*, manned by men from Plymouth and flying the flags made by the ladies of Devonshire. It was at that moment, and often again over the next few hours, that those on the bridge heard the unmistakable beating of a drum. The senior officers heard it too and couldn't understand it. Two searches of the ship were carried out for the mysterious drummer, who should have been at action stations. Nobody was found. The conclusion was that this had been Drake's Drum, but perhaps it was Blinker Hall, the great trickster, up to his tricks.

Chapter 6
Towards Bletchley

The legacy of room 40 was a powerful one, but little understood – and certainly little understood in the navy itself. The inter-war admirals had a vague idea that someone in their organisation had been jolly good at codes and assumed that this was some genetic factor found in the Anglo-Saxon race. Consequently, there was a vague assertion that, in any kind of cryptography battle, the British would always win. In fact, as I showed in my book *Operation Primrose*, the British naval codes were cracked by the German cryptographers – by Wilhelm Tranow and his colleagues – as early as 1935 and they continued to read the other side's naval signals, almost continuously, until 1943.

Once again, it was the crusty conservatism of the senior service which caused some of the difficulty. In the First World War, the cryptographers had been treated with some contempt by some senior officers at the Admiralty. Before the Second World War, the sea-going officers had shunned new telex-style wireless signalling equipment which would have given them some parity with Enigma, even if they could hardly read the Enigma messages of the other side.

But one reason why it was so little understood was the obsessive secrecy around the whole operation. Secrecy is vital in cryptography, but it has to be tempered with openness to the right people or there is no point in reading the other side's signals in the first place. These lessons were learned by Blinker Hall and his senior staff, but they were not widely put into practice. Successive attempts to write about Room 40 were quashed by the Official Secrets Act, wielded by William Clarke, who had risen to be one of the key figures in the Government School after the war. Even Hall's own autobiography was scotched half way through the process of writing it. Hall himself became one of a group of ultra-conservative diehard MPs in Parliament warning about socialism in industry.

Hall lived until 1943. He was available when Captain John Godfrey was appointed to his old position as Director of Naval Intelligence, another former battlecruiser commanding officer who found himself in the role, primarily because he had impressed Admiral Sir Dudley Pound by his breadth of literary knowledge. Hall lent him his flat in Curzon Street and provided Godfrey with regular advice. He was too old to return to work, but joined the Home Guard and remained a member until his death.

The main lessons about cryptography had been learned because those who had shaped Room 40 under Ewing and Hall stayed involved in naval code-breaking and were still there in 1939. After the armistice, there was a decision to merge the military and naval code-breakers in a new Government Code and Cipher School. This would form the basis of Station X at Bletchley Park, but the immediate decision about who should run it – Alastair Denniston from Room 40 or Malcolm Hay from MI1(b). Hay made the mistake of writing a tetchy memo, refusing to serve under Denniston. Denniston anyway played the cleverer game and was appointed, and he stayed in post until 1941. In response, Hay burned all the papers relating to the code-breaking activities of MI1(b), which is one reason why their work has remained so obscure.

So it was Denniston who led the negotiations with the Polish cryptographers for one of their Enigma machines and it was Denniston who shaped Bletchley Park until he was edged out after the fiasco of the memo written by Turing to Churchill. When he took over the School, Denniston appointed Knox, Clarke and Montgomery to work with him, and it fell to Clarke to defend the great secret, sending his vituperative memos around Whitehall warning of disaster. It was the former Foreign Secretary Arthur Balfour who mentioned it first, in a speech in 1925. Others who broke the secret included the journalist Filson Young, who was close to Beatty and set out Beatty's own view – a mistaken one – that the problem was non-naval personnel who had failed to understand the significance of the signals they were reading. Ewing himself dared to refer to the secret in an article in 1927 and was threatened with the Official Secrets Act by Clarke. The first book about Room 40, *40 OB*, by former Room 40 official Hugh Cleland Hoy, was dismissed as irrelevant. Clarke referred to Hoy as "a drunken typist"

During those same years, Hall leaked large numbers of decrypts to an American lawyer building a case for war crimes against the Germans. In due course, and through the legal process, they made their way to Germany where they had a profound effect. The discovery that their codes were as vulnerable as they had been caused shock in naval, military and diplomatic circles. Hall was also outfaced by a tactical move by the German government, claiming that the decrypts were forgeries in the hope that Hall could be persuaded to reveal more – he duly offered up the codebooks, revealing just how deep British penetration had gone.

It so happened, at the time, that the German military was considering future signals systems and the crisis persuaded them to adopt the Enigma method (though the German Foreign office always refused). It this peculiar roundabout way, the success of Room 40 led directly to the adoption of Enigma.

**

The question of how to use this unexpected source of vital information which Room 40 provided the navy was a very twentieth century problem, as it would turn out: how do you get information where it is most needed in highly complex, hierarchical and widely spread organisations? It was the central problem of twentieth century management, tackled in business between the wars in General Motors by Alfred Sloan, by creating a hierarchical divisional that made GM's structure a little like a fleet.

But even the development of modern hierarchical divisions failed to quite tackle the problem. The fleet was already structured along those lines, and it did not allow for the information to go the other way, from the front line to the top and back down again. It only allowed the top managers to send their messages and wait for obedience. As the navy discovered at Jutland, that failed to work as a solution.

Hall managed to combine extreme conservatism of outlook and attitude with serious and widespread innovation. He also seemed to grasp the practicalities of things and the Royal Navy, also based on the Nelson tradition of disobeying orders and the independence of command, also understood the importance of the wide spread of knowledge and the wide diversity of skills needed to make the most of it. Blinker Hall grasped this too, in the bizarre group of people he employed as cryptographers, and this was the approach to cracking codes which Denniston continued. He did so especially in the run up to the Second World War, when so many of the old hands returned to the fold and so many new young people joined them, including of course Alan Turing.

It is possible to argue – since the stakes were so high – that the failure to use signals intelligence effectively at the Battle of Jutland changed the world. If the Royal Navy had won their long-expected victory with the annihilation of the German fleet, it is quite likely that the German war effort would have collapsed, as it did when the navy mutinied in 1918. It would not perhaps have collapsed in time to save the British army from the disaster on the Somme, but it would have happened perhaps in time to save the Russians from the revolution and perhaps even to bring about a negotiated settlement rather than the threat to world peace represented by the Treaty of Versailles. Jutland would have been as famous as Trafalgar. Perhaps there would have been no Second World War. All this because the decrypts and the knowledge gleaned from them were not used as they could have been.

On the other hand, given that these mistakes were made, it was also possible for Hall to shift the way the signals were decrypted. Hall was able to take other opportunities from coded signals to bring America into the war and defeat the U-boat threat. It was also possible for him to shape the system that was put in place again in 1939, and by doing so to face down an even bigger threat. But that, as they say, is another story.

Acknowledgements and find out more

I am very grateful for all the help from the team at Endeavour Press, from Richard Foreman and Lydia Yadi, who are always so encouraging, and also to the staff at the British Library and London Library where I undertook most of the research. The papers of Denniston, Hall and Clarke are all at the Churchill College archives in Cambridge. I have tried to concentrate here on the books and sources which specifically cover Room 40:

Batey, Mavis (2009), *Dilly: The man who broke Enigmas*, London: Biteback.

Beesly, Patrick (1982), *Room 40: British naval intelligence 1914-18,* London: Hamish Hamilton.

Denniston, Robin (2007), *Thirty Secret Years: A.G. Denniston's work for signals intelligence 1914-1944. Polperro: Polperro Heritage Press.*

Bates, L. F. (1946), *Sir Alfred Ewing: A Pioneer in Physics and Engineering*, New York: Columbia University Press.

Gannon, Paul (2010), *Inside Room 40: The Codebreakers of World War I*, Hersham: Ian Allen Publishing.

Hoy, Hugh Cleland (1935), *40 OB: How the war was won*, London: Hutchinson and Co.

James, William (1951), *The Sky was Always Blue,* London: Methuen.

James, William (1955), *The Eyes of the Navy: A Biographical Study of Admiral Sir Reginald Hall*, London: Methuen.

Kahn, Daniel (1967), *The Codebreakers*, New York: Simon & Schuster.

Koerver, Hans Joachim (2007-9), *Room 40. German Naval Warfare 1914 – 1918,* Vols 1 and 2, Steinbach: LIS Reinisch.

Ramsay, David (2009), *Blinker Hall. Spymaster: The Man Who Brought America into World War I,* Spellmount: Stroud.

Tuchman, Barbara (1957), *The Zimmerman Telegram*, New York: Macmillan.

US National Security Agency (c 1960), 'The Room 40 Compromise', Washington, draft: https://www.nsa.gov/about/cryptologic_heritage/60th/interactive_timeline/Content/1960s/documents/19600101_1960_Doc_3978516_Room40.pdf

See also: Operation Primrose: U-110, the Bismarck and the Enigma Code (extract here).

It was Winston Churchill who coined the phrase 'the Battle of the Atlantic'. "Amid the torrent of violent events one anxiety reigned supreme," he wrote later, "battles might be lost or won, enterprises might succeed or miscarry, territories might be gained or quitted, but dominating all our power to carry on the war, or even keep ourselves alive, lay our mastery of the ocean routes and the free approach an entry to our ports."

Even Churchill's rotund expressions and mastery of language fails to quite do justice to the reality in mid-Atlantic, as freighters, tankers and liners were sent to the bottom in fire and burning oil, protected by an exhausted and dwindling fleet of destroyers and escorts, while increasing proportions of our imports lay in the ocean depths, along with their crews. It was a story of grit, daring, and frustration on both sides, and of long, tiring nights on watch from the sea-swept bridge of a corvette or a damp, freezing conning tower.

Meanwhile, ten more ocean-going U-boats were completing every month by the end of 1940, and the British ports were filling slowly with damaged merchant vessels that could not be repaired. In desperation, at the start of 1941, Churchill wrote a memo to the First Lord of the Admiralty, A. V. Alexander, the minister responsible for the navy, warning that cargo ships arriving in the UK that month were half those which had arrived the same month in 1940.

"How willingly would I have exchanged a full-scale attempt at invasion for this shapeless, measureless peril, expressed in charts, curves and statistics," he wrote later.

This was the reality that lay behind the desperate efforts to crack the Nazi Enigma naval code. Bletchley Park, the top secret wartime cryptography establishment, had its own stresses – but all those involved in the struggle to crack naval Enigma knew the stakes.

**

The performance of Benedict Cumberbatch in *The Imitation Game*, and the fascination with the life and work – and the untimely death – of Alan Turing, has tended to throw the spotlight onto the extraordinary and secret work by these Bletchley Park code breakers. The narrative has concentrated on how the Enigma codes were cracked, and due respect has been given to all those aspects of the puzzle that came together – from the original Polish pioneers who helped to find ways of reading the early versions of Enigma and passed on their insights, and their Enigma machine, to the British, to the teams working around the clock in an obscure country house in the middle of Bedfordshire, from Turing's leaps of imagination and the beginnings of computing, to the inspirational contributions made by his colleagues which made the various steps possible.

By far the toughest aspect of cracking Enigma involved the complexities of the naval code. The army and Luftwaffe versions of Enigma succumbed to the code breakers relatively early and signals were read with increasing ease. But the naval versions still held out, for reasons that will be made clear in this short book.

The purpose of it is to tell a small slice of the story – the capture of a naval Enigma machine from U110 and its immediate consequences – but also to tell the tale in the context of one of the most important months in the business of cracking the naval Engima code, May 1941. That month saw both the capture of U110, together with an intact coding machine, just a few days after the first breakthrough – the capture of the naval Enigma settings for June – followed by the crescendo of the Battle of the Atlantic only days later: the pursuit and sinking of the German battleship *Bismarck*.

But the book has a secondary purpose. That is to try and set the story of the Enigma code-breakers at Bletchley Park back in the context from which it has been wrenched, the huge operation around naval intelligence which embedded Bletchley and the code cracking enthusiasts in Hut 8 in a wider machine that tried to use what clues were available to protect convoys, and read the minds of the enemy.

And perhaps most of all, the purpose is to set this story in the most important context of all: the fact that German code breakers had – even before the outbreak of war – been able to crack the British naval code and, while Turing and his collaborators were wrestling with the sophisticated Enigma system, their opposite numbers at B-Dienst in Berlin (until heavy bombing drove them out to the small village of Eberswalde) were reading most of the signals between the British Admiralty and its ships and convoys at sea.

This is not to diminish the achievements of the Bletchley people, which led to a series of individual victories from the Battle of Matapan to the Battle of North Cape, when the battlecruiser *Scharnhorst* was sunk. Harry Hinsley, who worked there himself – and wrote the definitive study of British intelligence in the Second World War – argued that cracking Enigma brought the war to an end at least a year sooner, because the U-boat threat had been comprehensively defeated at the start of 1944, allowing the necessary troops and material to be brought across the Atlantic to make D-Day possible.

There is no doubt about the crucial role that Bletchley played in the victory over the Nazis, and especially over the U-boats. But it is important to balance what we know of the bursts of individual brilliance with the systems and community effort of naval intelligence as a whole, and as it actually was – a day by day, hour by hour struggle by two sets of intelligence machines and, in particular, two sets of brilliant code breakers.

Part of the purpose of this book is to draw together that struggle when it reached its height, during that crucial month of May 1941 – when the very survival of Britain hung in the balance – to work out why one side managed by the skin of their teeth to develop the advantages that they could use eventually to defeat the other on the high seas.

Operation Primrose is available from various outlets as a print or ebook

Other titles by David Boyle

Building Futures
Funny Money: In search of alternative cash
The Sum of our Discontent
The Tyranny of Numbers
The Money Changers
Numbers (with Anita Roddick)
Authenticity: Brands, Fakes, Spin and the Lust for Real Life
Blondel's Song
Leaves the World to Darkness
News from Somewhere (*editor*)
Toward the Setting Sun
The New Economics: A Bigger Picture (with Andrew Simms)
Money Matters: Putting the eco into economics
The Wizard
The Little Money Book
Eminent Corporations (with Andrew Simms)
Voyages of Discovery
The Human Element
On the Eighth Day, God Created Allotments
The Age to Come
What if money grew on trees (*editor*)
Unheard, Unseen: Submarine E14 and the Dardanelles
Broke: How to survive the middle class crisis
Alan Turing: Unlocking the Enigma
Peace on Earth: The Christmas truce of 1914

Jerusalem: England's National Anthem
Give and Take (with Sarah Bird)
People Powered Prosperity (with Tony Greenham)
Rupert Brooke: England's Last Patriot
How to be English
The Piper (fiction)
Scandal
How to become a freelance writer

Printed in Great Britain
by Amazon

BEFORE ENIGMA